Factoring
Case Studies

2nd Edition

Essential Lessons from
30 Real Factoring Clients

Jeff Callender

DASH POINT PUBLISHING

Federal Way, Washington

Factoring Case Studies
Essential Lessons from 30 Real Factoring Clients

by Jeff Callender

Published by:
Dash Point Publishing, Inc.
P.O. Box 25591
Federal Way, WA 98093-2591 U.S.A.

Website: www.DashPointPublishing.com

Library of Congress Control Number: 2012943558
ISBN: 978-1-938837-03-6 (Paperback)
ISBN: 978-1-938837-15-9 (PDF)
ISBN: 978-1-938837-21-0 (Kindle)
ISBN: 978-1-938837-09-8 (ePub)

Printed in the United States of America.

Dedication

To the Factors
Who Contributed to This Book

Contents

Preface 7

PART 1 SETTING THE STAGE 9
Introduction 11
   What This Book Is About 11
   How This Book Came to Be 12
Overview 15
   The Contributors 15
   The Case Studies 15
   Chapters Structure 17
   Icon Explanations 17
Contributors 21
   Jeff Callender 21
   Kim Deveney 25
   Melissa Donald 27
   Darrell Fleck 29
   Ryan Jaskiewicz 31
   Tony Neglia 33
   Rodrigo Riadi 35

PART 2 CASE STUDIES 37
1. Smallnhappy Graphic Arts 39
2. Blahzay Auto Transport 43
3. Dee Seetful and Associates 49
4. Shifty Shuffles Staffing Services 55
5. Hardluck Harvey's Homes 63
6. Claire's Repairs 69
7. Smallfrey Alarm Company 73
8. Razzle & Dazzle Manufacturing 79
9. Dunfore Day Care 85
10. Messner Janitorial Company 91
11. Budibuddy Metal Fabrication 95
12. Stalwart Security 101
13. Misfit Publishing Company 105
14. Sloppee Properties 109
15. Gogetter Property Services 115
16. Audacity Cleaning Service 119

17. Lunch & Munch Staffing 123
18. Dorrie Nobb Advertising 127
19. Clank Brothers Wiring and Cable 131
20. Hemisphere and World Loagistics International Transfer
    (HAWLIT) 137
21. Techie Trekker 143
22. Smuggley, Swindol & Finkbottom Finance 147
23. Onin's Workouts & Isometric Exercise Systems (OWIES)
    151
24. Mr. Scumbucket Janitorial Company 155
25. Safensound Janitorial and Maintenance 165
26. Slimegall Medical Transport 169
27. Methodical Manufacturing 175
28. Damon Deevyus, LLC 179
29. Battleground Janitorial 191
30. Effective Fundraising 197

PART 3 ANALYSIS 201
Assessment 203
    Good Clients and Bad Clients 203
    Factors' Vulnerability 209
    Factors' Mistakes 210
    Risk Minimization Strategies 212
    The Core of Factoring: People 214

PART 4 APPENDIX 217
Reference Charts 219
Acknowledgments 229
Important Notice 235
Also by Jeff Callender 236
About the Author 237

Preface

This is the fourth book in *The Small Factor Series,* which opens the door to the intriguing practice of factoring small business receivables. While you don't need to read the other books to understand this one, the purpose of *Factoring Case Studies: Essential Lessons from 30 Real Factoring Clients* is to educate and illustrate the many principles and instructions given in the other books.

The first book, *Factoring Wisdom: A Preview of Buying Receivables,* is a compilation of numerous short quotes from all the books that follow in the series, as well as other material I've written. It is a succinct summary of over 100 factoring topics, and provides an excellent introduction of what's to come. To get an idea of what factoring is all about, especially from the factor's perspective, this book is the best place to start. When you've completed the other books, returning to *Factoring Wisdom* is a great way to review what you've read.

The second title, *Fundamentals for Factors: How You Can Make Large Returns in Small Receivables,* provides the basic concepts from the point of view of the factor. *Fundamentals* describes what factoring is, how it works, businesses which can benefit, the remarkable returns possible, risks involved, and how to minimize those risks. It helps the reader define the meaning of "success," whether factoring is an appropriate move for his or her circumstances, and closes with a look at four small factors who enter the field from very diverse backgrounds, with quite different purposes.

The third book, *How to Run a Small Factoring Business: Make Money in Little Deals the Big Guys Brush Off,* is the "nuts and bolts" hands-on manual for running a small factoring operation. It includes first-hand lessons from the factoring industry, identifies where to find operating capital, provides marketing strategies, and describes numerous common mistakes small factors all too often make. There are chapters on due diligence, credit reports, reviews of factoring software, a sample factoring transaction from start to finish with an accompanying flowchart, and a many other resources available for small factors.

The present book, *Factoring Case Studies,* stands on its own and can be read apart from the others. Yet *Case Studies* provides those who have read the other books a large corner piece of the jigsaw of the factoring experience. This book gives flesh and blood to the crucial yet academic information imparted in the other volumes.

One can read the other books without this one and still become a successful small factor. However, this book describes in numerous, unique, and very personal ways what you're in for as a factor of small business receivables. Some of these stories will encourage – maybe even compel you – to enter the arena. Others might well scare you away. In either case, you'll find these case studies educational, revealing, thought-provoking, and even entertaining.

Jeff Callender

Part 1

Setting the Stage

Introduction

What This Book Is About

In the earlier books of *The Small Factor Series,* I included examples from my own factoring business to illustrate several points. Readers of those books may remember my very first client, the carpet cleaner whose receivables were literally piled in shoe boxes when we started. Organization was not his middle name, and unknown to both of us he factored several invoices that had already been paid when we began. Thus began my education as a small factor.

The purpose of that story was to give a real-life, human example in what was heavily information-laden material. While small factors definitely need the information to earn the high returns within their reach, they also need to realize how very human the experience of factoring is.

This is a people-centric enterprise. If individuals don't fascinate you, you probably will not find factoring very interesting. Exasperating at times – yes; quite lucrative at times – no question; but *interesting*…no. The purpose of this book is not only to illustrate and educate, but to share the fascination I find in factoring.

If you don't understand what people are really like deep down, the heavy dose of human nature you'll receive from factoring will be quite an eye-opener. I have found when you deal with people's money, you are handling something that over time reveals their inner nature. You will sometimes be surprised with what you find, as their outer facade is peeled away and the inner nature revealed.

Sometimes those surprises are pleasant and you find a true heart of gold; such moments and such souls are an honor to behold. Other times you expose a heart that is twisted and wretched, and you regret having been part of its unmasking. You also regret the loss of money and time, and the stress you experienced because of this person.

Peeling back that outer skin and revealing the inner nature is what this book is about. It's far more than just a book on alternative financing, though it is that as well.

How This Book Came to Be

One day I was speaking with a colleague who was having a seemingly never-ending saga with a very trying client. As the story unfolded into yet another unbelievable episode, I found myself thinking, "What an experience! The stories from this client alone could teach loads about the business of factoring. What would result if I could put together a collection of several true stories like this?!"

As that thought germinated I came to see that an album of stories from several colleagues would have great educational value. A group of stories – factoring case studies – would not only illustrate in human terms the principles, instructions, warnings, and suggestions made in the first books; it would be both fascinating and entertaining. Thus this book took its embryonic form.

I put together some thoughts as to what these case studies might include, and assembled a list of small factors I knew with solid factoring experience. I contacted these people and asked if they would be willing to share their experiences with clients for a new book. The response was strong and their replies made up the pages of the first edition of this book.

Several years have elapsed since publishing the first edition, and it's time to provide a second edition with completely new case studies. I again invited a number of colleagues to contribute to this edition, and the pages that follow share their experiences and wisdom. In this edition, I have written many of the case studies (which I didn't do in the first edition) so that a broader scope of material is provided. Hence we now have thirty case studies, whereas the first edition had twenty-one.

Each contributor was given the same instructions for writing his/her case studies. In short, I asked for "the good, the bad, and the ugly" of their factoring experiences. As you will see, each writes with a unique style and outlook. Below are the guidelines each contributor was given before sitting down to write.

For each case study, describe:

- How you and the client found each other.
- The industry the client is in, the client's product or service, and to whom the client sells.
- Why he/she wanted to factor, and why he/she wanted to factor with you.
- The approximate factoring volume.
- How you structured your rates, advances, and rebates.
- Why this particular client stands out from others.

For the "good" clients describe:

- What specifically made this a valuable client to you.
- How long he/she factored with you.
- What appealed to you when you accepted this client.
- What did/do you like about the client as he/she continues/d to factor.
- What features in him/her you look for in new prospects.
- If you were just starting to factor again, what you would do the same, and what you would do differently.

For the clients that were "bad" experiences, describe:

- The chronology of when and how things went south.
- Whether the problems were of the client's making and/or a result of your mistakes.
- What specific mistakes you made that you would do differently next time.

- Whether the client tried to defraud you, either intentionally or unintentionally, and if so, how.
- Whether the root of the problem was client mismanagement, incompetence, and/or personal problems/circumstances such as illness or divorce, etc.
- How your experience with this client has affected your procedures, general practices, or industries/clients/debtors you no longer accept.

Not one of these case studies is made up. Every story is true and each client is real. For the sake of anonymity, company names and personal names have obviously been changed. The names given them are monikers or acronyms which describe the essence of each person, business or experience in a few words. Hopefully they will bring you a smile or two, if not a good laugh.

With these preliminaries in place, let's look at an overview to help you understand the book's layout, the icons in the margins and their meaning, and the analysis that follows.

Overview

The Contributors

All the contributors to these case studies are honest-to-goodness, bona-fide smaller factors across the country. Their names are real and their companies are very much in business. Each has a unique background, is experienced in the factoring world, and has many valuable lessons to teach. The first chapter gives biographical information on each writer so you can get a better idea of their backgrounds, perspectives on factoring, and the positioning of their companies as factors. They are listed alphabetically by last name so you can find them easily for reference.

The Case Studies

Thirty case studies make up this book. Twelve of these studies could be considered good experiences, while eighteen are negative (and a few of those downright awful). Two client experiences were good for several years, but then something happened that made the relationship end badly. Six of the other bad experiences ended with the factor recovering most or all his/her funds. I want to point out this percentage of bad experiences does not reflect the proportion of good/bad clients in the portfolios of most factors. If it did, there would be very few factors in business!

All factors have a negative experience from time to time, but the vast majority of their clients and transactions hum along at a relatively smooth and steady pace. Make no mistake, however: the unpleasant ones are hard to forget!

The disproportionately high number of "lemons" is included here for instructional purposes. While you learn a great deal from good client experiences, you also learn plenty from the bad. That's why the negative case studies in this book are in such abundance. Their number is not intended to scare you away from factoring, but is included to give you several first-hand accounts of the troubling situations that can arise – and give you some handles on how to prevent them in the first place, as well as what to do once they're a full-blown mess.

Marketing is always a key issue for people starting a business. To help with this matter, below is a summary of the client industries included in these case studies (followed by the number of case study clients in each industry), as well as the marketing methods or referral sources the factors used to obtain these clients.

Client Industries:

Advertising	1
Alarm Installation	1
Auto Transport	1
Computer Programing	1
Day Care	1
Drayage Trucking	1
Electronics Importer	1
Foreclosure Restoration	2
Fundraising	1
Grant Writer	1
Graphic Artist	1
Home Restoration	2
Janitorial	5
Manufacturing	2
Medical Transportation	1
Metal Fabrication	1
Personal Trainer	1
Post Construction Cleanup	1
Publishing	1
Security Guard Service	1
Staffing	2
Wiring & Cable Installation	1

Marketing Methods/Referral Sources:

Accountant	1
Banker	3
Broker	12
Customer	1
Other Factor	7
Website	5
Written Article	1

Chapters Structure

Part 2 contains all thirty case studies. Each factor provides at least one case study, and each case study makes up a separate chapter. The case studies are not clustered by factor, but rather flow from one to the next in a logical progression of stories and lessons to be learned.

The words of all the case studies are those of the contributing factors. I have provided some editorial touches for clarity and added icons in the margins as running commentary. I have also changed the clients' company and owner names, added occasional footnotes, and provided closing comments of each case study. Thus this book is a shared effort between the contributors and myself.

Icon Explanations

Most pages have icons in the margin which point out positive or negative information described. Triangles and red flags are negative, while most others are positive. Below is a brief explanation and the ideas each icon conveys. If you're reading an ebook, bookmark the next page so you can refer to it as you read each case study.

Positive Icons

 Legal/Contractual Issue – A point of law or the factoring contract involving issues usually favorable to the factor.

 Benefit of Factoring – A benefit factoring provides the client is conveyed. Use these in your marketing!

 Desirable Feature – A desirable aspect of a client or customer is expressed. The more of these you find in a prospect, the better.

 Due Diligence – A standard due diligence activity is described

 Common Factoring Practice – A normal factoring procedure is being followed.

 Risk Minimizer – This is a precaution or action which lessens the factor's risk. Learn to weave these into your own practices

 Good Move– The action described will likely have positive consequences for the factor.

 Good Advice – So pay attention!

 Common Sense – One of the most vital assets of any factor

 Good Guy Wins – Proof that sometimes the good guy *does* win!

 Mark of Success – Experiences which make factoring gratifying for everyone involved.

Negative Icons

 Risk – The factor is taking a chance or the client is acting in a way which increases the factor's risk.

 Mistake – A mistake is being made by the factor, client, or customer.

If the error is the factor's, he/she is doing something he/she may regret later.

If the error is the client's, he/she is making a management decision (often without realizing it) that may prove costly to both the client and factor.

If the error is the customer's he/she is making a management decision that may prove costly to the factor.

 Over-concentration – The factor has too much money concentrated in this particular client, customer, or invoice. This can pose a grave danger to the survival of the factor's business. Alternately, the client may be over-concentrated in a particular customer, posing a risk to both him/herself and the factor.

 Bad Move – The action described will likely have negative consequences for the factor.

 Unbelievable!! – The action described is just hard to believe.

 Not Fair – Proof that life is not always fair and the good guy *doesn't* always win.

 Red Flag – When these come up…watch out!

 Fraud – The client has committed a fraudulent act. Very, very bad.

Contributors

Jeff Callender

Dash Point Financial Services, Inc.
www.DashPointFinancial.com

Tacoma, Washington

Case Studies Written
1. Smallnhappy Graphic Arts
3. Dee Seetful & Associates
6. Claire's Repairs
9. Dunfore Day Care
12. Stalwart Security
14. Sloppee Properties
15. Gogetter Property Services
21. Techie Trekker
24. Mr. Scumbucket Janitorial
26. Slimegall Medical Transport
27. Methodical Manufacturing
28. Damon Deevyus, LLC
29. Battleground Janitorial
30. Effective Fundraising

Jeff Callender grew up in Riverside, California, and graduated from Whittier College near Los Angeles. Jeff has been involved in factoring since January, 1994 when he began as a broker, working in that capacity for about seven months. He then ran his own small factoring business. Several years later he worked for a large national factoring company for about a year as an Account Executive. He started Dash Point Financial in 2001.

Dash Point Financial specializes in purchasing receivables of very small businesses; all clients start at or under $10,000 in volume and grow from there. Dash Point funds transactions in various industries, except for trucking, construction and third party medical receivables.

Jeff is also the President of FactorFox Software, LLC, which provides the cloud-based software platform, FactorFox. The database is used by many factors of all sizes both in North America and around the world, and provides many additional services to its subscribers.

Don D'Ambrosio

Oxygen Funding, Inc.
www.OxygenFunding.com

Lake Forest, California

Case Studies Written
- 2 Blahzay Auto Transport
- 7 Smallfrey Alarm Company
- 22 Smuggley, Swindol, & Finkbottom Finance

Don D'Ambrosio grew up in Philadelphia and graduated from Temple University with a Bachelor's degree in Business Administration focusing in Accounting/Finance.

Prior to starting Oxygen Funding, Don was employed over 11 years with BNC Mortgage, Inc., a Lehman Brothers subsidiary, where he was Corporate Controller and Chief Financial Officer. He was responsible for all financial aspects of BNC Mortgage including budgeting, forecasting, proforma planning, financial statement preparation, cash flow analysis, taxes and external audits from CPA firms and regulatory agencies.

Don started Oxygen Funding in 2007. His company provides cash to qualified clients with short term cash flow needs through the purchasing of secured and reliable accounts receivable. The Company looks at a client's profile rather than just an industry. Preferred clients have monthly volumes of $100k and below with room for growth.

Kim Deveney

American Funding Solutions LLC
www.funding4you.com

Blue Springs, Missouri

<u>Case Studies Written</u>
10. Messner Janitorial Company
17. Lunch & Munch Staffing

Kim Deveney is a graduate of the University of Missouri - Columbia, receiving a BS in Accounting. She earned her Master's in Business Administration from Webster University in Kansas City. She worked as accountant for State Street for 11 years before starting American Funding Solutions LLC in August of 2003.

Kim started American Funding Solutions LLC, in Blue Springs, Missouri. As managing partner she has helped numerous small businesses improve their cash flow with factoring. American Funding specializes in small ticket factoring transactions of services to various industries, except for construction and third party medical factoring. Kim has a passion for helping small businesses and is a proud member of the International Factoring Association. She is a founding member of The Factoring Alliance LLC which helps to educate and promote factoring to the small business community.

Melissa Donald

LDI Growth Partners
www.ldifactors.com

Walnut Creek, California

Case Studies Written
13. Misfit Publishing Company
19. Clank Brothers Wiring and Cable
25. Safensound Janitorial and Maintenance

Melissa Donald spent the first eleven years of her career working in and then managing a commercial collection agency. In 2001, she left the collection industry and took a position with a factoring firm in Walnut Creek, California. During her tenure, Melissa worked her way from a Senior Account Executive to Operations Manager to Vice President of Operations.

In January 2007, Melissa and her two partners launched LDI Growth Partners. LDI works diligently and intentionally to increase awareness of the benefits of factoring for businesses in all stages of growth. They work side by side with clients to create tailored factoring programs that fit their unique needs.

LDI Growth Partners works with clients in all stages of growth, and focusses on businesses in the early stages, generally from start up to about $1M-$2M in annual sales. While not industry specific, LDI works with many contractors and trades people who are working with banks and real estate brokers to rehab homes after foreclosure. LDI's portfolio includes businesses of all types, from the neighborhood florist (account debtors are funerals homes) to cutting edge technology companies who are using factoring to bide time and increase the valuation of their company before taking on venture capital.

Darrell Fleck

RMJ Capital Inc.

Colorado Springs, Colorado

<u>Case Study Written</u>
8. Razzle & Dazzle Manufacturing

Darrell Fleck graduated from Southern Illinois University, Carbondale. For 24 years he served as General Manager for Dunkin Donuts/Baskin Robbins. Following that position, for five years he was President of Abbott Fire and Safety, a business to business company with around 7,000 business clients.

He recently concluded nine years' volunteer service as board member of Ronald McDonald Charities of Southern Colorado. He is also past Chairman of the Board of Adopt a Village International, a charity which connects people and resources to humanitarian needs around the world to end the cycle of poverty.

Darrell is a Managing Partner in RMJ Capital of Colorado Springs, Colorado. RMJ Capital is a niche alternative financing company focused on the financial needs of small to medium size companies across many industries.

Ryan Jaskiewicz

12five Capital, LLC
www.12five.com

Oakbrook Terrace, Illinois

Case Study Written

11. Budibuddy Metal Fabrication

Ryan Jaskiewicz is CEO of 12five Capital, LLC. He graduated from University of Illinois at Chicago with a Bachelor of Arts in Political Science with an emphasis on international politics and economic policy. He grew up with factoring as his father is a 25-plus year veteran of the industry. Ryan recognized his entrepreneurial drive early and taking the knowledge he learned from his father, started his own factoring firm in early 2006 at the age of 23.

12five provides working capital to small and medium size businesses. It specializes in high growth companies with annual revenues between $100k and $10m. Its goal is to provide financing that is simple, easy, and straightforward to clients, so they can truly understand where their company is positioned and what it will take to grow.

Ryan is married and lives in Riverside, Illinois. When he's not factoring, you can probably find him running the Salt Creek trail, as running marathons are his other love, next to his wife.

Tony Neglia

Stonebridge Financial Services, Inc.
www.stonebridgefs.com

Brentwood, Tennessee

<u>Case Studies Written</u>
5. Hardluck Harvey's Homes
16. Audacity Cleaning Services
18. Dorrie Nobb Advertising

Tony Neglia graduated from the University of Pennsylvania in 1986 with a bachelor's degree in mathematics. He started his career as an actuary in Philadelphia, and his job took him to New York, Paris, Japan, Australia and London. After twenty years in the actuarial field, Tony settled in Brentwood, Tennessee in 2004 where he currently resides with his wife and two children.

Tony began as a factor in 2006, starting Stonebridge Financial Services. He specializes in factoring small companies and will purchase invoices as low as $200, with volume as high as $50,000 per month in most industries, with the exception of construction, third party medical, and trucking. Tony is active in the factoring community and has has served on the Board of Directors of the International Factoring Association.

When he is not busy servicing Stonebridge clients he can be found at the Nashville Chess Center where he serves on the Board of Directors as its Treasurer. He also volunteers at local schools promoting and teaching chess to children of all ages in the Nashville area.

Rodrigo Riadi

Front Range Factoring
www.frontrangefactoring.com

Westminster, Colorado

Case Studies Written
4. Shifty Shuffles Staffing Services
20. Hemisphere and World Logistics International Transfer (HAWLIT)
23. Onin's Workouts & Isometric Exercise Systems (OWIES)

Originally from Chile, Rodrigo Riadi holds an Engineering degree from Universidade de Sao Paulo, Brazil, and a Master of Business Administration from the Tuck School of Business at Dartmouth College in Hanover, New Hampshire.

Before founding Front Range Factoring, Rodrigo first worked in asset management for Unibanco in Brazil. He then worked for Lehman Brothers in New York, where he advised companies on mergers and acquisitions across a wide range of industries. He then held a strategy and business development position at Capital One Financial, where he managed the sale of Capital One's family of Mutual Funds to Fidelity.

He started Front Range Factoring in June, 2010. The company's focus is on small businesses and startups with less than $25k per month in factoring needs.

Part 2

Case Studies

1.

Smallnhappy Graphic Arts

Jeff Callender
Dash Point Financial

Arianna Artiste is a graphic designer who owns Smallnhappy Graphic Arts, which creates various kinds of artwork including printed ads, catalogues, brochures, packaging graphics, and logos, as well as website design. She factors one larger customer who sells exercise equipment and inflatable furniture. She found my website using an internet search and has been a steady client for about three years.

 Arianna started factoring because her customer, while a steady and dependable payer, takes 30 – 45 days to pay. Her other, smaller customers pay with cash or credit cards, but she needs to get paid sooner by her largest customer to meet regular expenses without falling into arrears. She chose Dash Point because our web site makes clear we specialize in funding very small businesses of her volume, and she had difficulty finding other factors who would consider her. She is a one-person business and likes to operate alone, with manageable volume, and isn't much interested in growth. She runs her business to fit her lifestyle: she wants to create her art and enjoy what she does. Like many artists, making big bucks isn't that important to her.

 Her small volume and lack of projected growth made her undesirable to larger factors. Since Dash Point accepts clients factoring less than $10,000 to start, this approach both fit her needs and appealed to her. My business model is to fund very small businesses; their growth, while welcome, is not my top priority. Thus Arianna and I felt a certain kinship as we started – two small business owners working together to do what we most enjoy.

Her beginning credit limit of $10,000 has not needed to be increased, since her factored invoices pay in about 30 to 45 days. Invoice sizes are consistently a few hundred to a couple thousand dollars apiece. Her customer regularly sends payment to my lock box. When invoices occasionally stretch to about 50 days and haven't paid, a short email or phone call results in a check being sent right away. While having one customer increases my risk with this account, the fact that her invoice size and factoring volume are both pretty low (and won't increase) mitigates the risk. If she were to lose the account and couldn't pay me back (not likely since we maintain an escrow reserve), my loss would be small. She also has other customers she doesn't factor which provide income for her.

I like this account because even though the volume is pretty low and there is little chance for growth, invoice submissions are steady, the account is low maintenance, and my income (while relatively small) is consistent, low-risk, and dependable. When we occasionally need to talk to Arianna, she is always pleasant and responsive. She meets her paperwork submission deadlines regularly and we have never had a problem with her account.

Comment

This is precisely the kind of very small client that small factors like. The positive aspects of this account:

- Steady factoring with consistent volume.
- Low risk.
- Non-factored accounts produce other income, providing her company stability.
- This is a dependable, organized business owner who is pleasant to work with.

While this account wouldn't appeal to larger factors because of the low volume, the low income it generates, and little likelihood of growth, it's great for a small factor like Dash Point. Even though more work may be involved with many very small clients, having a portfolio full of accounts like this is still pretty easy and provides an excellent spread of risk.

If given the choice, I'd take ten very small, low maintenance clients like this over one bigger client with erratic dependability, questionable quality of work, and lack of integrity, any time. The next four case studies give a taste of what clients like that can be like.

2.

Blahzay Auto Transport

Don D'Ambrosio
Oxygen Funding

The mission statement of most factoring companies is to assist prospective clients with cash flow by purchasing their outstanding invoices. This is a rather short but all-encompassing statement that covers a broad range of topics from finding a prospective client to funding that first invoice. At our company we believe that as important as sales are to the bottom line, proper due diligence and the preservation of capital is just as important. This case study will show how important it is to have your due diligence performed correctly to protect your factoring company.

A few years ago a prospective client, Blahzay Auto Transport, owned by Jay Blahzay, was referred to us from a broker. The prospect, located out of state, was engaged in the business of transporting cars cross country on big auto transport trailers. His debtors were several well-known car manufacturers with household names. His business was growing and he needed cash flow to hire additional employees and take on more jobs.

As much as we would like to fund every prospect that comes to our company, there are several extremely important questions that every factoring company should ask early in the due diligence process:

- How long has the client been in business?
- Can they provide current financial statements and tax returns?

- Are any UCC-1 financing statements in first position on the client?
- What is the credit history of both the client and account debtor?
- How is the client's company organized?
- Can the client provide an aged invoice schedule for the customers they would like to factor?

These are just a few samples from our company's due diligence checklist. Depending on the type of industry being factored, a factoring company's checklist may vary. In our experience, gathering these documents can take anywhere from two days to a few months. Much of the process is dependent on the willingness of both the client and customer to provide the information requested in a timely and presentable manner.

After gathering the required documents on Blahzay Auto Transport, we moved forward with our proposal. Jay accepted our terms and we proceeded to fund his invoices. For the first month or so we were able to verify, fund, and collect without any problems. The client's business was growing and he was looking for us to increase his credit line so we could purchase more of his invoices. However, in the second month of funding our team noticed several invoices with one of his customers were still outstanding.

This development struck us as odd since this particular customer was very strong and the invoices with his other customers were paying in a timely fashion. We contacted Jay so he could shed some light on the situation and he informed us that he was not aware of any issues with the customer. We followed up with his customer, who surprisingly informed us that they had never changed the payment address to our office even though they signed our notice of assignment.

A "Notice of Assignment" is generally a written instruction to the client's customer that the client's accounts receivable have been assigned and are payable to the factor. This is an extremely important document for factoring companies. This document protects the factoring company in the event a payment is accidentally sent to the client instead of the factor. Even if the client skips off with your money, this document ensures you are still owed the funds from the client's customer. Hopefully, you will never have to enforce this notice, but having it as part of your due diligence requirements before funding is imperative.

As it turned out, the client received our checks and actually deposited the funds directly in his company's account. Believe it or not, this happens quite often in the factoring business. Many times, the client's accountant or bookkeeper will deposit everything that comes into their office without knowing which check is the property of the factoring company. With this knowledge, we informed the client that all factored funds were the legal property of our company and needed to be returned to us immediately. Our factoring agreement has a clause that specifically addresses misdirected payments. It basically imposes a huge penalty on the client if the funds are not returned to our office within a twenty four hour period once the client has been notified.

The client informed us he wouldn't be able to return the funds to us for another week or so. He also stated that since it wasn't his mistake he had every right to the money to take care of a few expenses, and pay us later. We explained to him this was unacceptable since he had .now been paid twice for his invoices, and informed him of the misdirected payment clause in his agreement. He brushed it off saying we would get our money in about a week or so. Finally, we informed him of the notice of assignment which he and his customer signed when we opened his account with our company. We also mentioned that his customer would be receiving a demand payment letter from our legal department explaining the situation and how they owed us the money for the invoices he deposited.

This was not the way we wanted the situation to play out, but unfortunately Jay left us no other choice. If this demand letter to his customer (a legal document) had reached the auto company, he would ave been portrayed in a very negative light, and his relationship with them would have been severely damaged. Needless to say, we received our funds from Jay (along with the penalty) the next day. We also ceased funding him because we felt that when given the choice to do the right thing, he chose not to do so.

A colleague of mine compared the due diligence process to putting together a puzzle that never gets fully completed. You try to get as many pieces of the puzzle to connect in order to form a clear enough picture to move on to the next step. In the race to get every deal funded, you will find many factors will try to slow the process for very good reason. Unlike banks and other secured lenders, factors advance cash to qualified clients based on a piece of paper in the form of an invoice. Sure, the returns are high but so is the risk.

The learning lesson from this case study: always have a notice of assignment perfected with all customers to ensure any misdirected payments will be paid to the factoring company.

Comment

I never cease to be amazed at how blasé so many clients can be when they receive a check for factored invoices, and deposit the check without much thought. Moreover, when they have been told this action is completely unacceptable, many still consider converting checks as no big deal – even after being clearly told they just committed fraud. We'll see clients in other case studies who do exactly the same thing.

Jay Blahzay is not unusual at all in his thinking, though such an attitude makes factors gray very quickly. His mindset – "since it wasn't his mistake he had every right to the money" – is appalling to any factor. He couldn't have been more wrong, and Don had "every right" to show him the door. I have had clients (not included in this book) who after being soundly educated as to what to do with checks they receive for factored invoices, continued to deposit future ones anyway. Incredible.

As you will see in many other case studies that follow, clients converting checks, as Jay Blahzay did, is a very common experience among factors. When it happens, some factors immediately cut off the client, as did Don, while others continue working with the client for a variety of reasons. As you will see, this is an issue for which you must be prepared. Have a written policy in place, and give (and verbally review) it with every prospect before signing the contract. Impress upon every new client the gravity of such actions with explicitly clear instructions: *don't do it.*

But count on it – many will anyway.

3.
Dee Seetful and Associates

Jeff Callender
Dash Point Financial

This case study is an example of how any business owner, including one you would think would have some integrity by virtue of the business he or she is in, can still deceive and cheat you – even for a small amount of money.

Dee Seetful and Associates was owned by a woman in the deep South who provided grant writing, 501-C3 certification for non-profit agencies, and training and mentoring for people starting their own business. She had a number of clients in her area and regularly counseled business startups, providing one-to-one coaching and frequent classes to those who were beginning non-profits companies. Dee's business appeared to be fairly well known in her community, especially among those in need of her services. She provided regular classes on such topics as bookkeeping, marketing, correctly following non-profit guidelines and requirements, and even business ethics.

Dee was referred by a larger factor for whom her receivables volume was too small. I started her with our usual $10,000 line of credit and normal rates. Her first factoring schedule included two invoices for grant-writing services to a small non-profit agency in her town named Dinkyrink Development. The owner of Dinkyrink was a personal friend of Dee, as well as a business customer. One invoice was for $2,700 and the other for about $6,100. With our 80% advance and 5% deduction put into her escrow reserve fund, the net advance was about $6,600.

While larger non-profits are usually creditworthy and safe to factor, smaller ones can be a bit tricky because you usually don't know how financially stable they are. Credit history is typically lacking, and should problems arise and you end up in court, a for-profit factor may seem like a bully to a judge who is sympathetic to a small non-profit agency. Because the amounts were small and Dee had a good history with this customer who had always paid her consistently at 30 days (as her payment agings showed), I approved the schedule and funded the advance at the end of December.

A couple weeks after funding, Dee emailed me that the invoice should pay the first or second week of February, which was consistent with Dinkyrink's payment history. When we hadn't received anything by mid-February, I emailed Dee asking for an update and she emailed back that she was checking into it.

A week passed and we still had not heard back. We decided to call Dinkyrink directly and speak to the owner, Lizzie Toobizzy, to ask her what was going on. We were informed by the person who answered the phone, Marcie Mastiff, that Lizzie was in a meeting and unavailable to take the call. We requested she return the call, which didn't happen. We continued to make follow-up calls and each time Marcie answered and informed us Lizzy was in a meeting.

We informed her of our purpose for calling and asked if anyone else there could help us. Marcie told us that Lizzie was the only person who could deal with Dee Seetful's invoices. This seemed a bit odd, but considering she was the owner of a small non-profit, made some sense. We were beginning to get frustrated, though; we were getting nowhere and Lizzie Toobizy did not return our calls. Apparently Lizzie or Marcie informed Dee that we had called, because Dee promptly called one of my staff and clearly informed her she did not appreciate our contacting her customer directly.

By early March no payment had arrived and we turned back to Dee, telling her of our difficulty getting paid by her supposedly good-paying customer. We reminded her the delay was costing her in factoring charges that were continuing to accrue. She was aware of that but I didn't detect a note of concern in her voice; after all, she had received her advance. As sometimes happens with clients, once they get their advance they may not exhibit a sense of urgency that we get paid back. I had the feeling that she viewed this as my problem, not hers. Not showing concern about increasing discounts is a sure red flag that something is wrong. Anyway, Dee had been in contact with Lizzy and gave a deadline of Friday, March 25 for Dinkyrink to pay the overdue invoice. She told us of this deadline date and it appeared we would finally get paid.

On the following Monday, another person in my office called Dinkyrink to see if the check had been sent. She actually spoke with Lizzie Toobizy directly, who told her a check for about $3500 had been mailed to Dash Point, and the call ended. While we were glad some funds were on their way, the amount seemed odd since neither invoice was for that amount – one invoices was smaller, the other larger. Why was this amount paid? I continued to call Dinkyrink and had trouble getting past Marcie Mastiff.

Calling Dee to find out about the odd invoice amount and remaining balance got nowhere – she didn't answer the calls and her voice mailbox was full. Now there was no way to get through to her or even leave a message. I continued to press Marcie about the remaining balance and was finally informed that just before our check was to be cut by Dinkyrink, Dee had informed their bookkeeper – whom I wasn't even aware was in the picture – to pay Dash Point $3195 (which he did), and pay Dee the balance because her bank account was overdrawn and she "needed it." The bookkeeper, who had not been made aware by Lizzie (to whom the NOA had been sent) of any relationship with Dash Point, did as instructed. Dee received the check, deposited it, and completely ignored us from that point on. She apparently decided she was done with Dash Point and ceased contact. She decided when she misdirected the payment that our getting the remaining funds was going to be our problem. She was right.

We then sent Marcie a copy of the NOA Lizzie had received by registered email. We did not require signed NOAs at that time as long as we had the registered email providing it had been opened – which legally is all that is required. I asked why Lizzie Toobizy had allowed such payment over notice and Marcie indicated Lizzie had no recollection of receiving the NOA. I didn't doubt that for a second (Lizzie always seemed too preoccupied to do much of anything helpful) and I told Marcie her agency was now liable to pay the remainder of the bill to Dash Point, despite having already paid Dee.

At that point Marcie indicated she was a paralegal and she didn't see how that could be possible. I briefly educated her on UCC law and how payment over notice very certainly had put her agency in risk of paying the amount twice (unless Dee paid us back). I also said I was amazed that Dee would jeopardize her business by defrauding us for such a small amount. Marcie said she felt the same way and stated her agency would no longer do business with Dee. However, she said she needed to consult with the agency's attorney, Neville Knozsquatt, before saying anything more, and ended the conversation.

When I didn't hear from Marcie after a few days, I gave the account to my collection attorney, Cleaver Squeezem. He decided to first contact Neville, and upon doing so, learned Dinkyrink Development obtained his services via Prepaid Legal. Not surprisingly, Neville Knozsquatt knew nothing about UCC law. After several attempts to deal with Neville, Cleaver felt pursuing Dinkyrink Development was not going to accomplish anything. He made a several attempts to contact Dee Seetful but was never able to reach her. Because of the relatively small amount involved, Cleaver advised us he couldn't do anything more and we should just write it off as bad debt.

I felt the debt was still collectable and gave the account to a collection agency we use, who are not attorneys like Cleaver is. That agency, Onus, Dred & Trembal, takes a more direct approach: they send an investigator to go to the office of the person owing money, who tries to collect using verbal persuasion. That is, the investigator makes clear the funds are owed, suggests the negative repercussions if they don't pay, and hopefully inspires the person to pay what is owed. Sometimes this approach works, sometimes it doesn't, just as Cleaver's approach of warning they face a lawsuit: sometimes it's effective but not always.

In this case, after several unsuccessful attempts to talk to Dee in person, the investigator gave up in frustration. Dee was either never in the office or would not come out of her office to speak with him. Like Cleaver, collectors Onus, Dred & Trembal gave up in both frustration and consideration of the relatively small amount owed. We finally wrote off to bad debt our remaining unpaid advance, about $3,400.

Dealing with Dee Seetful was a lesson learned that people are not always what they seem. Sadly, that's true for those who work with small start-up companies and non-profits...and even teach classes in business ethics.

Comment

Any time a bill is late being paid, especially from a dependable customer, and the client does not appear concerned about the delay (which means they're paying you more), something is wrong. In this case, I have no doubt that Dee Seetful intended to redirect part of the payment because her bank account was overdrawn and she "needed it." So of course she wasn't worried about it – she knew exactly what she was going to do: steal the payment due me.

The kicker in this case study is that Dee made a living of teaching non-profits and other small businesses how to get started and run their companies following the requirements and laws of the land. Incredibly, this respected woman – who taught courses in business ethics, among other things – didn't have the slightest qualm about diverting funds due her factor. Her own needs came first in her mind, and unfortunately that is usually the case with clients. When clients have their backs against the wall and must choose between doing what they perceive as necessary for their business to survive, and being sure the factor gets paid properly, they will almost always choose the former.

Obviously the type of business a client is in gives the factor no assurance they will be honest in such situations. If any type of client should have been honest here, it would be Dee, especially for such a relatively small amount of money. But this case study shows that factors cannot assume a particular client will do the right thing because it is the right thing. The need for money trumps what is right just about every time.

This is also true with very religious (and very unreligious) individuals. I have worked with numerous church people over the years who wear their faith on their sleeves, "talk the talk," and go out of their way to make clear they have been saved. Unfortunately, when push comes to shove, in many cases, the need for money overcomes the desire to do the right thing and they have left me holding the bag – if not outright defrauded me, as Dee did.

My ebook, *Top 10 Illusions about Risk and Loss*, contains a chapter that speaks specifically to this issue. It's called "Illusion #8: There is Less Risk Factoring People with Strong Religious Beliefs. *Alternate:* There Is More Risk Factoring People with Strong Religious Beliefs." That chapter is worth the read if you think someone is trustworthy based solely on outward appearances.

I have learned from these experiences that a client's type of business, position in the community, or personal faith has no bearing on whether they will be honest. In the long run, these mean nothing when it comes to predicting who will do the right thing.

4.
Shifty Shuffles Staffing Services

Rodrigo Riadi
Front Range Factoring

Shifty Shuffles Staffing Services was referred by a broker and provided healthcare staffing to a few national accounts. With high margins, weekly payroll and customer terms from 30 to 45 days, factoring made sense. The company was operated primarily by Willie B. Wiley who had extensive experience in the industry, having owned a previous business performing the same services to some of the same customers. Willie's prior company also factored its receivables.

Initial due diligence of Shifty Shuffles and debtors showed promise, despite some yellow/red flags. Debtor companies had mostly sparse credit histories, but further investigation revealed enough good credit in their corporate families to make me initially comfortable. Customer contracts with Shifty Shuffles Staffing Services were clean with little room for claims or refunds.

As I learned more about the company, I found it was owned by Willie's parents, Miley and Riley Wiley, who had clean backgrounds. Willie himself had a few judgments and a minor criminal offense. Since the company was a startup, there was no track record.

According to Willie, the company he previously owned had factored its receivables for over a year. The relationship with the factor had ended several years ago, so the UCC on that company was expected to expire soon.

However, it did not become fully clear under what circumstances the factoring relationship ended, but Willie made it plain he did not want to use that factoring company again. Willie stated he had started a new company under his parent's ownership to access their savings for startup capital, and to avoid any issues with the previous factoring company.

I sensed risks surrounding the existence of a previous factoring relationship and the company's ownership structure. I could not obtain documents from Willie to clarify the story as to what had happened with the previous factoring relationship. This can be a major red flag, since concerns regarding a factoring company can indicate issues such as fraud or debtor problems.

The fact that Willie operated the company largely on his own but was not the owner was also cause for some concern. His father Riley supposedly performed some of the accounting but was not visible running the business. I spoke with both Miley and Riley to understand their individual roles, confirming that most of the business was in Willie's hands, which they corroborated.

Several factors contributed to my perception of mitigated risk.

1. Willie's livelihood appeared linked to the industry. The company's owners, his parents, had good backgrounds. Willie was in his 40's and had a family with children. I perceived these facts as lowering the likelihood of fraud.

2. The relationship with the previous factor was almost five years old and had ended over two years earlier. That relationship existed with Willie's previous company which had different ownership (Willie) from the current company (his parents). I perceived this length of time and difference in company ownership as putting enough distance between

potential past issues and a current factoring relationship.

3. Good debtor credit and relationship. As mentioned earlier I was comfortable with the credit of the debtor, Easley Foold Nursing Facility. I made Willie a proposal which was accepted after some haggling. After the contract was signed, the debtor was notified. During conversations, the debtor appeared to be experienced with factoring, acknowledging the notice of assignment and being flexible as to invoice verifications.

4. It also became clear from those conversations the invoicing process required by Easley Foold Nursing Facility and the reports they generated would give us enough information to closely monitor all activity. On Mondays, Willie invoiced the debtor, cc'ing me. Later that week, Easley Foold would send a confirmation email referring to that week's invoice. Then on Monday of the following week they would send another confirmation email. These reports were a regular part of the debtor's payables process, and they agreed to copy us when they were submitted.

During the first several months Front Range funded the account, and everything ran smoothly. I received checks every Monday referring to invoices issued around 30 days prior. Willie added new customers and everything ran well with them as well.

However, over the course of a few weeks Willie lost some of his placements, apparently due to his late payments of their contractor fees. He did not hide any of this from me, and I tried to help him organize his finances. He was receptive to the idea but never followed up.

One week I did not receive the usual confirmation email from Easley Foold Nursing. The following Monday I contacted them, and was told there had been a misunderstanding on their part; but everything was fine now and they sent the reports. However, I did not get a check that week as expected. I contacted Easley Foold again, who became increasingly resistant to communicating with me. What's more, Willie became impossible to reach, not responding to voice mails or emails.

After repeated attempts I spoke with Easley Foold, who was quite defensive at first, and became confused with our conversation. They agreed to help clarify the issue however, and we escalated collection efforts with them internally for that purpose.

After several communications, Easley Foold agreed to again direct payments on outstanding invoices to Front Range, but initially wanted me to resolve the misdirected payments with Shifty Shuffles Staffing. After this, another payment was surprisingly misdirected, and it took several more communications with Easley Foold to get them to redirect payments to Front Range again. I was able to talk to Willie once or twice throughout the process, and he dismissed everything as a series of misunderstandings. Willie's father Riley appeared confused, but cooperated very little.

I only learned what happened through bits and pieces of information that was assembled together after the fact. It became clear that Willie had told Easley Foold the factoring relationship with Front Range had ended. Further, all payments should be directed to another company (Phonyphront Inc.) who was now handling the staffers that had been placed with the Easley Foold. Willie also told Easley to please not speak with me. In a separate, terse, communication to me copying the debtor, informed me to not contact Easley Foold for any reason (apparently with the intent of gaining time).

Easley complied with the redirection notice from Shifty Shuffles Staffing, without asking further questions at the time, and issued payments to the new company, Phonyphront Inc. In the coming weeks, we had the opportunity to speak with the owner of Phonyphront, Ima Patsy, who basically "cashed" the checks received from Easley to Willie. Ima seemed quite puzzled over what was happening.

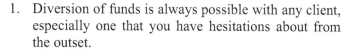

Realizing we would not go very far with Willie in recovering the misdirected funds, we concluded we had a strong enough case to try to recover the misdirected funds from Easley Foold Nursing Facility.

It took many weeks of communication with Easley. When we approached 60 days overdue for the first invoices that were outstanding, we mentioned that our next step would be to engage collections attorneys. Shortly thereafter they agreed to settle the amount outstanding in exchange for a release. We received the check, issued a release, and closed the account.

Lessons

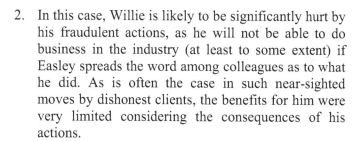

1. Diversion of funds is always possible with any client, especially one that you have hesitations about from the outset.

2. In this case, Willie is likely to be significantly hurt by his fraudulent actions, as he will not be able to do business in the industry (at least to some extent) if Easley spreads the word among colleagues as to what he did. As is often the case in such near-sighted moves by dishonest clients, the benefits for him were very limited considering the consequences of his actions.

3. The loss of some of Shifty Shuffles' staffing placements due to late payments should have raised a red flag that prompted me to terminate the relationship. It is possible, although debatable, whether such termination would have produced a better outcome.

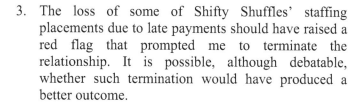

4. Communication is a key factor in recovering funds in a situation like this one, where litigation can be avoided.

On paper this account was profitable, but it gave us lots of headaches and wasted much time.

Comment

This client relationship began on a rather uneasy basis. Willie started his company under his parent's ownership "to access their savings for startup capital, and to avoid any issues with the previous factoring company." If his parents supported his business endeavor, would he still not have "access" to their capital if he owned the company? Why couldn't he just start the company in his own name and borrow money from them? Plus he wanted to "avoid any issues" with his previous factoring company. What issues was he trying to avoid? Rodrigo was never really told.

If anything doesn't pass the "smell test" early, this is it. Clearly Willie was hiding something right from the start. Who would like to bet he pulled some kind of fraud with the previous factor, and therefore wanted to keep Rodrigo from contacting that factor? Better for Willie to keep his new factor in the dark.

Another mistake Rodrigo made here was assuming that because Willie was in his 40's and had a wife and children, this lowered the likelihood that he would commit fraud. Assuming someone will be honest because he has a family is just as erroneous as assuming someone will not defraud you because she teaches classes in business ethics, as we saw in the previous case study with Dee Seetful. You might as well think someone won't defraud you because the person has brown eyes. Be clear: *anyone* can cheat you. Anyone.

We also see in this case study a familiar pattern observed in other negative case studies in this book:

1. Things go well at first.
2. A change in regular payments occurs.
3. A too-easy explanation is made (in this instance, a "misunderstanding" occurred).
4. Payments still don't appear as they should.
5. The customer becomes resistant to contact by the factor.
6. The client becomes uncommunicative and difficult to reach.
7. Misdirected payments happen (and continue) and the factor is defrauded.

In other words, the factor is kept in the dark by the client as to what the client is doing (fraud by various methods), and only learns about it or figures it out after the fact.

One of the purposes of this book is to help you identify patterns that accompany fraud, and thus recognize them when they are in the process of happening. Yet such recognition is often difficult because the client is quite crafty and clever at concealing what he's doing, plus usually the factor doesn't want to suspect the client of doing something so wrong.

In this case, Willie went to the extent of bringing in Ima Patsy to cover and even further enable his fraud. As is often the case with crooks, innocent outsiders are utilized to provide an appearance of legitimacy (often to a debtor). Yet fraud is fraud no matter how it's perpetrated, and sooner or later the factor learns what's going on. Unfortunately, it's often later.

Further, any time a client tells a debtor not to speak to the factor, and especially tells the factor not to speak with the debtor "for any reason," the client is simply up to no good. As the factor who owns the receivables, unless you have agreed to a complete non-notification relationship, you have every right to contact a debtor any time you feel the need.

Never let a client dictate your actions in this way. You, the factor, must be in control of the relationship. This case study (and several others) show what can happen when you aren't.

5.

Hardluck Harvey's Homes

Tony Neglia
Stonebridge Financial Services

Hardluck Harvey's Homes provided renovation and lead abatement services for low income residents in the state of New Hampshire. The owner, Harvey Hoodwinker, was referred by a broker. While the state funded these projects, they outsourced the management of these programs to third parties. The structure was fairly complex involving multiple community action agencies and a consultant.

All of the funds from the state were funneled through one of the community action agencies who then distributed funds to the other community action agencies. Hardluck Harvey's Homes did work for two of the community action agencies. A consultant, Chelsea Checkonum, was hired by the state to make sure that the work was completed properly by the contractors.

 In retrospect, I did not initially understand the flow of money from the state through the community action agencies. I was primarily concerned that the work was completed and that all invoices were verified with the state hired consultant.

Everything was working quite well the first six months or so. This is a critical time for us when trust is established with our client. After this initial trust had been developed, Harvey submitted a few invoices (about $30,000 worth) for an agency that I had not previously factored.

63

At the time I did not notice the customer's name on the invoices did not match the name of customer Harvey entered in the factoring administrative system we use. In other words, the customer's name on the actual invoice was ABC, but the name of the customer that Harvey entered into the factoring system was XYZ. As was the procedure for this client, we verified with Chelsea Checkonum, the state's consultant, via telephone the work was completed and the invoices were all approved for payment.

After the invoices aged for some time we started asking Harvey and Chelsea about payment of these invoices. Ordinarily we ask someone in the A/P department of the account debtor, but since our relationship was with Chelsea we asked her first. Since she did not handle invoice payments she referred us back to Harvey.

Over time, Harvey became less and less available and came up with more and more unbelievable excuses. First his son was in the hospital because he broke his hand. Then Harvey's cell phone broke. Then he couldn't respond to our emails because his wife kicked him out of the house, took his laptop computer and he was sleeping in his truck at the job site. Then since he had nowhere to live he couldn't complete the contracting jobs and decided to move upstate to live with a friend. His friend was going to give him work so he could pay us. Harvey even gave us a (phony) email address and/or telephone number so we could contact his friend to verify. Not much came of this.

We realized we needed to contact the account debtor directly to find out the status of the late payments. This is when we learned how many entities were involved and how money was moved from the state through the various agencies. When we finally contacted the correct agency and inquired about the invoices we were told that one or two had been paid weeks earlier, but another was about to be paid. We were also told the checks for the paid invoices were picked up personally by Harvey. This is when we realized Hardluck Harvey was a crook.

Nevertheless, the fact that Harvey picked up the payments was irrelevant. If he had not picked up the payments, we were told they would have been mailed to him anyway. We informed them that we had notified them that the invoice payments were assigned to Stonebridge and emailed them a copy of the Notice of Assignment (which was even signed). Much to our dismay, we were informed that the NOA was signed by someone at a different agency and the agency to whom I was speaking was under no obligation to pay Stonebridge.

While we weren't entirely convinced this was a different agency it was clear that we needed to get a new NOA out to them quickly (and all the other agencies that were previously notified). This was especially important since this agency was about to make more payments to our client. This time we sent the NOA's via certified mail.

A few days later we tried contacting the agency but now they were avoiding us. In retrospect, we believe they paid Harvey for the remaining outstanding invoices. We then contacted the supervisor of the person to whom we had previously been speaking. Fortunately, he took our call, called in his employee and put us on speaker phone.

We explained to them the meaning of the NOA. We further explained that they do not have to agree to pay to Stonebridge. The fact that they have been informed of the assignment requires them to make payments (for invoices from our client) to Stonebridge. We also suggested that they send the letter to their in-house counsel for confirmation of what we were telling them. However, I asked that they make sure the attorney from whom they seek counsel is familiar with the Uniform Commercial Code (UCC). We also reminded them that if they make any further payments to Harvey this will not relieve their obligation to pay Stonebridge and they may have to pay the invoices twice.

They assured us that Hardluck Harvey's Homes was no longer working for them and there would be no further payments anyway so this was a moot point. Remember, Harvey also told us he couldn't even complete the jobs he was doing so this information matched somewhat to what the agency was telling me.

However, another issue emerged. Chelsea Checkonum, the consultant who had been very cooperative throughout this process, told us that Harvey had been doing more work for the state. In fact, he was even doing work for the same agency that had paid him directly!

A couple weeks after speaking with the agency that, we believed, paid over notification we started contacting attorneys in New Hampshire. Our case was too small for them but they gave us the names of collection attorneys who might be able to help.

The same day I spoke with the attorneys, I received a call from the agency in question. They informed me they had a check for $38,000. The reason they were calling was that they wanted to know if they could give some of it to Harvey so he could continue working. I told them to give him $5,000 but made it clear they had to send the rest to Stonebridge.

They told me they would have to inform Harvey he was only getting $5,000 out of the total $38,000. I wished them luck reaching him because I couldn't reach him for months. Five minutes later I received a call from Harvey. I told him how nice it was to hear from him because I was worried sick about is son, his wife, his broken phone, his sleeping in his truck, etc. Despite the fact that he had clearly defrauded me and I was out quite a bit of money because of his actions, he wanted to know when he would be getting his rebate and escrow reserve returned! (He is still waiting.)

In retrospect I did not fully understand the cash flows for this account until things went south. Having a clear understanding of this is very important for new clients, especially those working for any level of government in which payments do not come directly from the branch for which they have done work. We are now much more careful about understanding the relationship of all the parties involved, how the cash flows, and we ALWAYS make sure the account debtor's name on the invoice is the same as the name our client enters in our administrative system.

Comment

Every now and then you have an account in which a seemingly remarkable series of misfortunes strikes an unlucky client. While such things certainly can happen, when they get to the point they are "unbelievable" as Tony put it, they probably are. People who divert checks and otherwise steal funds you are due can be remarkably creative in the stories they come up with. Often there is an element of truth to these stories, but such people have a way of embellishing them to make you feel sorry for them, just like Harvey Hoodwinker. It didn't take long for Tony to learn that this spinner of tales "was a crook."

Another telling fact about this case study is that as Harvey's fraud extended over time, he became harder and harder to reach. Again, this is a classic, extremely common move by someone who has done something dishonest. The less they have contact with you, the harder it is for you to pin them down and find out what really happened. Factors usually end up getting the truth from almost anyone *except* the dishonest client. We'll see this in numerous other case studies involving fraud by the client.

Something else to keep in mind from this case study is the complicated flow of funds, which can sometimes be the case with government receivables. Not completely understanding this flow, Tony sent his NOA to the wrong agency, who correctly told him they weren't obligated to honor the NOA. The lesson here is, be sure you understand exactly to whom the NOA needs to go, and get it right the first time. If you don't you may have a mad scramble like

Tony did to get it right; in the worst of circumstances, even then it could be too late. Tony was fortunate he was able to make this correction, and that he had Chelsea Checkonum giving him updates he would never have received from anyone else. She may be considered his angel in this case, letting him know Harvey was still working and getting paid through the very channels that should be paying Tony.

One final observation. Notice Tony said, "…we tried contacting the agency but now they were avoiding us. In retrospect, we believe they paid Harvey for the remaining outstanding invoices." As we'll see in other case studies as well, debtor avoidance often means they've paid the client and don't want to face you. When this happens to you, consider it a blaring alarm warning you to act *now* (not later) to take whatever action necessary to get your money back.

6.

Claire's Repairs

Jeff Callender
Dash Point Financial

Claire's Repairs, owned by Claire Stedfast, is a client who found Dash Point Financial's website about three years ago while searching for a factor. Her company rehabs older homes in need of repairs which are owned by lower income people. Claire factors to meet payroll and keep her cash flow steady to pay her operating bills.

Claire lives and works in Philadelphia, and the city provides funds for these renovations. While this business is very similar to the previous case study, Hardluck Harvey's Homes, the payment process is much simpler in Philadelphia than in New Hampshire.

Claire receives an order for a renovation, agrees to the price, and her crew does the work. When the job is complete, the work is inspected by a city official and signed by both the inspector and homeowner. She submits a copy of the signed approval document, and payment from the city agency responsible for the project is typically made about 45 to 60 days following submission of the paperwork.

Unlike the previous case study with New Hampshire, Philadelphia's funds come directly from the city agency for whom the work has been done, and payments go right to my lock box without any issues. Claire has never tried to misdirect funds and has been a very straight arrow to work with. She is cooperative, appreciates how factoring keeps her business going, and I have never had any serious difficulties with the account ever since she started factoring.

A nice part of working with Claire's Repairs is every couple weeks the city agency administering the program provides a list of upcoming invoices that are scheduled to be paid. It includes the invoice numbers, payment date, and payment amount for each invoice scheduled. The city provides this list to Claire who faxes it to me, giving a quite dependable list of when all her factored (and unfactored) invoices will be paid. Occasionally a payment doesn't arrive when the list says it should, but a phone call or email usually provides a corrected list the next time around. While the list is not always 100% accurate, it's close enough to give us a good idea of when we'll be paid for almost all her factored invoices.

Invoices typically range from about $2,500 to $8,000. Her volume has fluctuated from a low of about $5,000 to $40,000 per month; most of the time her outstanding receivables are in the $15,000 - $50,000 range. As with all our clients, we maintain an escrow reserve account which is used from time to time when an occasional invoice payment is delayed or less than expected. She ran into a tax issue at one point but between her steady factoring and a good balance in her escrow account, she has never fallen into serious arrears with us.

I like working with Claire because she has proven to be an honest, steady client with good volume, a good debtor, and a regular list of when we are going to be paid. The city's checks always come to us and while they're a bit slower than they used to be, there is never a worry that the checks won't clear.

Comment

Notice many of the same words that keep appearing which describe good clients:

- Steady
- Consistent
- Honest
- Cooperative
- Appreciative
- Good communication
- Good volume
- Dependable
- Good debtors
- Reliable payments

All of these describe Clair, and these words should be on the description list of any factor prospecting for new clients. If you find a prospect who appears to match all of these descriptions, do your best to close them.

Just remember, things can go south on you rather quickly (as we'll see in the next case study). They can even go south with a formerly good client you've had for a very long time (as we'll see in Case Study 26, Mr. Scumbucket Janitorial Company).

So never let down your guard.

7.

Smallfrey Alarm Company

Don D'Ambrosio
Oxygen Funding

Smallfrey Alarm Company, owned by Leon Little, found us through our website and completed our online application. The company was engaged in the business of installing alarms in commercial buildings which included card readers, relay switches, and indoor and outdoor security cameras. At the time of our proposal Leon was looking to fund approximately $50,000 per month which qualified him for an advance of 80% and a factoring discount of approximately 4% for 30 days.

After several discussions with Leon we proceeded with our preliminary due diligence. When we first opened the file we noticed there were several UCC-1 financing statements filed by other factoring companies. A UCC-1 financing statement is a legal form that a creditor files to give notice that it has an interest in the personal property of the debtor. A UCC-1 filing is not necessarily a negative indicator when detected during the due diligence evaluation process. In many instances, the prospect may have a loan with a financial institution or leased equipment which has prompted the bank or leasing company to file a security interest against that company. However, multiple UCC-1 filings from other factoring companies should always be a cause for concern.

Depending on the date of the filings it usually falls under one of two scenarios. If the filings are more than six months old, the prospect may have utilized the services of another factoring company and has since terminated the relationship. In some instances, you will find that financial institutions forget to remove their UCC-1 filings even though

DD

they no longer have a security interest against that company. On the other hand, if the UCC-1(s) have been recently filed by other factoring companies it usually indicates the prospect may be shopping for a new factoring company. Many factors immediately place a security interest on a prospect upon the receipt of a completed application. The reasoning behind this procedure is to have secured first position on all collateral prior to the initial funding.

Our company's position is to proceed cautiously whenever a prospect is shopping multiple factoring companies simultaneously for their business. Obviously, it is good for a prospect to seek multiple offers since they will be looking for the best price and service. However, as a factor, you do not want to conduct a complete evaluation only to find you were being used as a counter bid against another factoring company. This practice can be both time consuming and costly depending on your due diligence procedures.

Eventually we approved Smallfrey Alarm Company as a client. We found Leon had utilized a factor several years ago but had to cancel the relationship due to the slowdown in the economy. For good measure we contacted the previous factor who assured us there were no issues with our new client other than the slowdown in his business. The previous factor also mentioned they could not start a new relationship with Leon since his monthly factoring volume would be well below their minimum requirement. Also, as we had suspected, this factoring company forgot to remove their UCC-1 filing.

With our security position perfected, agreements signed and invoices verified, we proceeded with our first funding. For several months, the process of verifying and funding went off without a hitch. To Leon's credit he agreed to allow us to withhold additional escrow reserves since he was restarting his business. This would prove to be a very good move as you will see later.

So what could go wrong with Smallfrey Alarm? After all, his invoices were paying in a timely manner and his funding requests growing. Also, Smallfrey's customer, Stonewallen Megacorp, established open communications with us and we easily verified the invoices. The following will serve as a series of red flags that led us down a path we never intended to travel.

The first red flag started with the aging of Smallfrey's invoices. The terms between our client and Stonewallen were 45 days. Typically we were paid somewhere around the 50th day since Stonewallen was located on the east coast and we are on the west coast. Sometime around day 60 we placed a call to Stonewallen who informed us the invoices were placed on hold for payment; we would need to contact the project manager, Walter Alter, for further details.

We immediately contacted Walter who felt we needed a conference call with their legal team to discuss several issues regarding our client. As a funder, the last thing you want to hear from the company paying you is that they want to discuss your client's invoices with their lawyer. That was red flag number two. Later that week we had the conference call and were informed by Walter they would not be paying us on any of the outstanding invoices. Their reason for nonpayment was due to a problem with the work performed by our client on the last phase of the project. According to Walter, the work performed by Smallfrey was substandard and they had to hire another firm to fix the problem and get the project back on schedule.

We immediately contacted Leon regarding this situation, and he agreed there were several issues on the later stages of the project because Walter Alter – the *new* project manager – kept changing the work orders without sufficient notice. This forced his crew to work through the night on several occasions. He also maintained the work was performed within the specs of the contract and there should not be any issues.

Within a few weeks we received formal documentation from Stonewallen's attorneys, Stickittooem & Bulleys, stating they would not only be withholding payments on all outstanding invoices, but they would also be requesting restitution for additional amounts they had to pay to the new contractor to remedy the final phase of the project. At this point, we just assumed it would be best to cut our losses and move on. Before closing the book on this entire fiasco, we had our legal team review the contract to ensure we weren't missing anything on our end. Fortunately our team found specific wording in the contract that stated any work disputed by the contracting company must be in writing to the contractor within 10 days and the contractor had the right to remedy and work under dispute.

We brought this information to Stonewallen's attention to which they responded by requesting a myriad of documents including all invoices paid from inception to date, copies of our client's contractor license, etc. Obviously they were stalling and looking for a loophole. Finally after several months of back and forth between lawyers they came back with their findings. According to Stikittooem & Bulleys, Smallfrey Alarm was operating under an alarm contractor's license when it should have also been operating under a general contractor's license.

Our legal team disagreed, stating he was operating under the correct licensing and did not require an additional general contractor license. Our legal team then advised me this was a gray area if it went to court and we stood about a 70% chance of winning the case. However, per the agreement, the loser was on the hook to pick up the winning party's legal costs. For us, this would cost us five times the amount that was owed to us for the outstanding invoices. As a small factor, this fight was basically a David versus Goliath confrontation. It was so frustrating knowing we were in the right but did not have the deep pockets to take on this fight. In the end, we wound up settling the case and actually saved our client the additional restitution Stonewallen was seeking for paying an outside contractor to complete the project.

Lessons learned from this experience are as follows:

1. Completely verify all invoices and get the approval in writing when possible.

2. Stay on top of all outstanding invoices and react quickly when any payment patterns fall out of the norm.

3. When working with any contractors, make sure they are current on their licensing and be sure that they have the correct license for the specific work they are performing.

4. Whenever possible, maintain escrow account reserves for potential bad debts.

5. Maintain strict credit limits so you do not overexpose yourself to one client.

To conclude, this case study did not involve fraud or any type of illegal behavior by either our client or the account debtor. This was an actual dispute by two parties with us, the factor, caught in the middle. In the end, the disputed amount was manageable and we had reserves on the client which cut our losses in half. It was definitely a learning lesson for our company. Fortunately, we were able to learn from it and move on to fund another day.

Comment

This case study shows that a factor can lose money without being defrauded, and can lose money when neither the factor nor the client has done anything wrong. This was, as Don put it, a "dispute by two parties with us, the factor, caught in the middle." When a large debtor's aggressive attorneys are involved, that's not where you want to be.

Don made some good moves here. The fact that he called the customer about 10 days after payment was expected but not received, alerted him to a problem right away. Had he let this go and simply waited longer before calling, which is easy to do, the problem would have been delayed and made worse.

Further, when making such a follow up call and being told the payments were placed on hold, you know right away you have a problem. Having to speak with the project manager, then their attorneys, further confirms this. He wisely brought his own attorneys in.

As we have seen from earlier case studies, dealing with someone's attorney often means you're likely to incur some serious expenses trying to recoup your money. Even though this case didn't go to trial – it would have been quite risky and potentially far too costly for Oxygen to have done so – Don was in something of a no-win situation no matter what he did. Under the circumstances Don came out about as well as he could have hoped in this situation, though he still incurred a loss.

This is yet another lesson in the statement, "Don't expect the legal system to protect you." Too often it protects only those who have the most money to pay attorneys.

8.
Razzle & Dazzle Manufacturing

Darrell Fleck
RMJ Capital Inc.

 To help protect us from fraud, 100% of our clients are from direct referrals and/or introductions. To do this we spend a good amount of time networking with business leaders, lawyers, CPA's, and bankers. Often bankers or bankers between jobs are the best referral sources. They see many loan proposals that are not approved by banks and thus are perfect candidates for factoring. We have found that all referral sources have short memories, so regular contact is critical.

A banker between jobs named Rich S. Hunter brought us Razzle & Dazzle Manufacturing. Razzle & Dazzle created and patented a product which is currently exclusively sold to the U.S. Government. They outsource the vast majority of the manufacturing process, with only assembling done in house. When Razzle & Dazzle was presented to us they were a $1,000,000 per year business that had been factoring with an out of state factor for about a year. They were constantly at odds with their factor, Confounding Funding, due to the complicated contractual relationship.

Confounding Funding charged discount fees by the day and had a moving reserve, based upon the total amount outstanding as well as the days outstanding. In addition Razzle & Dazzle had problems understanding which factored invoices had been paid and which were still open. During a casual conversation between Rich and the principles of Razzle & Dazzle, one of the principles complained about their factoring relationship – which provided the perfect opportunity for our banker to tell them about RMJ Capital.

We asked Rich to set up a face-to-face meeting with the owners, and to retrieve all of the relevant financials and tax returns. Within two days we met in their office. The benefit of such in-person meetings in their place of work is that we gain a much better feel for the clients, their operation, and size by "having a tour." This is a rarity for us, as many of our clients are out of state, and we have to use other sources to confirm the businesses' story.

During our meeting with Razzle & Dazzle we discovered a number of items: some good and some not so good.

On the not so good side:

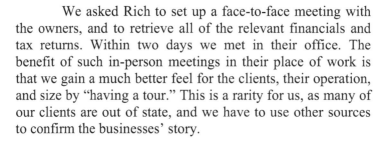

1. We were dealing with an unusual ownership structure. The business was owned by a fairly recently divorced couple, with the ex-wife's new husband now working in the business as well. Thus, we were dealing with the divorced husband, Rusty Razzle, the new husband Dusty Dazzle, and their mutual (ex-) wife, Ruby Razzle (now Dazzle). This was a business with only one other employee. Needless to say worth further understanding.

2. No inventory was kept in stock, they were manufacturing strictly to order, and yet were behind on paying their own manufacturer, Makesfurem Manufacturing. Where was the cash going?

3. Razzle & Dazzle would be a long term factoring client as they not only had to get current with money owed Makesfurem, but they also needed to pay themselves and build up inventory of their product.

4. Ruby handled the bookkeeping and sounded like a MBA/CPA/lawyer when she presented numbers and described the financial accounting of her company. But in reality, she had no clue as to their complete financial position. All she really knew was how much

money (she thought) was in the bank account after checking online that day.

5. We heard endless stories about problems with Confounding Funding, all of which told us they didn't really understand their current advance, discount, and reserves terms. They were clearly very frustrated with the process.

6. Razzle & Dazzle was struggling to pay their manufacturer, Makesfurem Manufacturing, who couldn't afford the raw materials needed unless they were paid quicker by Razzle & Dazzle.

On the good side:

1. Razzle & Dazzle was factoring 100% of their invoices.

2. Razzle & Dazzle was looking to double their business in the coming year, which means even more of a cash squeeze if they didn't factor.

3. Although Razzle & Dazzle had only one customer (increasing risk if they lost the account), the customer was the federal government.

4. While many factors worry about creditor concentration, we know although the government might be a pain to deal with, they do pay their bills.

5. The government had a password protected web site where we could track all invoices, status of payment, and acceptance of bills.

6. The government's website also controlled the ACH payments, and through password protection, protected RMJ Capital from payments being diverted.

After the tour with Rusty, Dusty and Ruby and hearing where their pain was, we reviewed our program and made sure we emphasized how we could meet all of their needs while eliminating their pain. We described our flat discount rate that based upon net 30, which would not have any other charges till the invoice hit 61 days. We reviewed our report, available to us at any time which we email weekly, showing every open invoice as of the time on the report. We showed them how simple it is to submit invoices and explained our wire would include all excess reserves. We talked about how to improve their bookkeeping, the need to build up capital and then invest in inventory, and assured them we could manage working with the government. They were sold on the spot!

We set up our standard factoring agreement. We outlined how their reserve is calculated and balanced each time new invoices are factored. We also explained the discount rate based on the government's 30 day payments, and our paying an ongoing commission percentage to the person who referred them.

Following our discussion, we reviewed their business plan and goals, and discovered their manufacturer, Makesfurem Manufacturing, might also be a prime candidate for factoring. Through Razzle & Dazzle we were referred to Makesfurem and met with them regarding their own cash flow needs. We determined by cleaning up Razzle & Dazzle's receivables and through factoring with RMJ Capital, Razzle & Dazzle would be able to pay Makesfurem quick enough to solve their cash flow squeeze. We were an instant hero to Razzle & Dazzle and to their main supplier, Makesfurem Manufacturing.

    Since starting to factor with us, Razzle & Dazzle has more than doubled their business since they are now focusing on sales rather than cash flow, with all invoices being net 30. Because of the secure website, we know every invoice's pay date – prior to our purchasing – and have yet to have a single invoice go past 30 days. Our broker, Rich S. Hunter, has been making about $20,000 per year from this one client. Needless to say, he is always on the hunt for other clients for us.

 Rusty, Dusty, and Ruby continue to look for other markets to sell to while continuing to develop new products. This is a perfect example of a factoring company helping a small business grow, and enabling business owners to sleep at night rather than tossing and turning, worrying about cash flow.

Comment

This client's company includes a very odd mix of business and personal relationships – a man, his ex-wife, and her new husband – as equal business partners. In many companies this unusual triad could have caused very serious problems, but fortunately in this case it did not. However, as you look for prospective clients, be aware that uncommon personal relationships like this in a business can make things complicated, if not quite risky.

This company's primary issue appeared to be a cash flow problem, despite the fact they were already factoring. Even though Ruby could rattle off numbers and sound like an "MBA/CPA/lawyer when she presented numbers and described the financial accounting of her company," she really knew nothing more than someone who just looked at their bank balance online. As a result, they couldn't pay their supplier on time, the principals were not paying themselves, and they kept no inventory in stock. As Darrell insightfully asks, "Where was the cash going?"

Ruby didn't know, and all three of them blamed their first factor for everything. The reason that factor was the "bad guy" came down to this: they didn't understand how their advance, discount, and reserves were calculated or charged. This is probably why Ruby's financial thinking was so muddled and explains why the books were in disarray. Ruby didn't know how to record anything that involved the factor – which was just about everything.

If Darrell could provide easily understandable factoring terms, they could know what their true factoring costs and advances were, and move forward on far better footing. Fortunately, that's exactly what he did and thereby created a win-win-win-win situation – for the client, supplier, factor, and broker.

As we see in this example (and in Case Study 28, Damon Deevyus, LLC), when a factor's rates and charges are convoluted and complicated, the result is often a client who is confused, unhappy, and unable to run the financial part of the business very well. Therefore, make a point of keeping all your factoring rates simple and easy to grasp. The more complex your rates, advances, and reserves, the less your client will understand what you're doing and what they're paying. This can lead not only to running a business blindly as Ruby was, but very soon, distrusting and blaming you, the factor, for everything. That's the last thing you want.

Keep your rates simple and you'll be doing your clients a service that many factors – for reasons that make no sense to me – just don't provide.

One last thing. One of the best aspects of this client is the information available to Darrell on the government's website. He knew every invoice's pay date *prior* to purchasing, and has yet to have a single invoice go past 30 days. Debtors who provide this kind of information make your life as a factor extremely easy when it comes to risk analysis and follow up. Any time you have access to such a web site, utilize it and be thankful you have a client whose debtor provides you with this extremely valuable information.

9.

Dunfore Day Care

Jeff Callender
Dash Point Financial

Dunfore Day Care, owned and operated by Viki Tim, was a child care center in Chicago. Viki was referred to Dash Point by a friend of hers who ran a day care center in another state who factored with me. Factoring helped her friend's business quite a bit, and Viki was eager to start factoring in order to meet payroll and grow her business, just as her friend had.

Most of Dunfore's children were from low income homes, whose day care costs were paid by the state of Illinois. While no invoices were involved, every month she submitted detailed records of each child for whom the state paid the number of days each child attended. This was submitted on a form the state provided and Viki turned in at the end of each month. The state would then pay her about three weeks after the end of the month according to her submissions.

However, because she had payroll twice a month, waiting three weeks after the end of the month meant she had no funds to meet the two previous payroll periods; this is why she needed to factor. Because she had no official paperwork to give me until the month was over, I created a spreadsheet on which she kept a running tally of each child's attendance, the daily amount the state paid for each child, and the calculation of the total payment by the state for the first two and last two weeks of each month (when her payroll was due). We used these spreadsheets as a temporary substitute for the official sheets turned in to the state, until the end of the month when she provided those to corroborate what she had entered on the spreadsheets.

This procedure involved a lot of trust on my part that what she entered on the spreadsheets was what she would submit to the state, and then in turn what the state would pay. While the work was done prior to advancing, the official form (the equivalent of an invoice) would not be turned into the state until a bit later. She started small so my exposure in the beginning was relatively low. I knew factoring would greatly help her business and she strongly wanted to make it work, so I didn't have a sense of high risk with her account, though clearly some risk existed. This would take close monitoring; but I knew it would be quite lucrative for both of us as her business grew.

The first few months of factoring went well, and the state indeed paid according to her spreadsheets and the official forms she turned in. She was able to meet payroll without any problems, and over the next few years her business grew and flourished. After about three years of factoring the number of kids in her care had tripled, she expanded into a nearby building, hired more staff, and the business was going great guns. Her spreadsheets were working perfectly, the state was paying dependably, and she became one of my best clients, producing excellent income for Dash Point. At the height she was factoring about $60,000 a month, we were paid without incident, and everyone was happy.

Unfortunately dark clouds started gathering at about year four. As the economy worsened, the state of Illinois' financial position became much more than troubling. It developed one of the worst budget deficits of any state in the country, was way too many billions of dollars in the red, and became slower and slower paying its vendors. At first Dunfore continued to be paid in a timely fashion, but gradually the state's payments became smaller and smaller and they were no longer paying the full amounts owed. Because we were giving her an 80% advance we were able to get by with the smaller payments, but the payment rates continued to drop, so we lowered her advances to 70%, then 65%. When the state's payments fell below that threshold, we had a very serious problem.

Since she didn't have any other factorable clients or invoices she could use to replace the state's short payments, and we burned through her once-healthy escrow reserve just trying to stay even, her account became seriously in arrears. She didn't have the funds herself to make us whole, and every time we funded her, the debt just became larger since the state's payment was smaller than the time before. As long as the state continued paying this way, we were in a death spiral.

The decreased advances just barely met her expenses. She laid off staff, lowered the number of kids on her rolls, and tried to get by. Still the state's payments shrank, and finally stopped all together. We had no choice but to cease funding her, which in turn forced her to close the business. She tried to run the day care from her home with a small number of kids and no state payments, but it was too late. She declared bankruptcy, and that was that.

One of my formerly best clients was gone and my total exposure when she closed was about $30,000. We gave the account to collections to try to get whatever they could from the state, but that went nowhere. Given her bankruptcy, the state's huge deficit, and the number of other and much larger vendors owed huge amounts by the state, it was a complete loss with no hope of recovering anything.

This was a tough one, and the client had absolutely no responsibility for what happened. She ran her business as she always had – and according to the state's guidelines, as she was supposed to. Likewise, she had been an excellent client for me: cooperative, prompt and dependable with her paperwork, never dishonest. Viki was simply a victim of the recession and Illinois' economic mess. She held no hard feelings toward Dash Point when we stopped funding her, but her life has become a struggle without her business.

Looking back, I realize if a few things had been done differently the ending might not have been so difficult. First, Viki's business was heavily overconcentrated with the state as her primary payer, and far too dependent on its payments to run her business safely. She needed to have other sources of revenue – a higher portion of payments from parents, perhaps another related service to generate additional income – *something* besides the state of Illinois. Like any business, a heavy concentration in one customer can lead to a bitter ending, even if that concentration is with a state or other government entity.

Second, though it would have been difficult, when I saw the writing on the wall and realized the state's payments were not going to improve, I should have pulled the plug and stopped funding her much sooner. While this would have forced her to close her doors earlier, my exposure would have been less and my write off smaller. For her, the result would have been the same anyway: in either case she would have been out of business.

This experience, plus the regular news of other states, cities, and counties being in severe financial crises of their own, has made me extremely cautious about accepting state and local governments as debtors. No longer the slam dunk they once were for paying their bills, we must now be very cautious and learn the economic health of any level of government we fund. Times have changed for factors, along with everyone else.

Comment

This is the kind of situation that breaks your heart. Here was a great client who played by the rules and did everything she was supposed to do, and with whom both the client and factor made excellent income together. But through no fault of Viki's, the business became a nightmare for herself, her employees, the families of the kids she served, and her factor. Even if I had pulled the plug earlier (which would have been better for me), all it would have done for her was force her to close sooner. Truly a no-win situation.

The take away? When you see the writing on the wall with a problem client or debtor – especially a government with serious financial problems – don't hesitate to terminate the relationship sooner rather than later. It's not an easy decision, but it can certainly be the wise one.

The next case study is an example of the factor recognizing this very risk, and fortunately making the decision to end the relationship before it got out of hand.

10.

Messner
Janitorial Company

Kim Deveney
American Funding Solutions

Fess & Les Messner, father and son owners of Messner Janitorial Company, saw an article I wrote for the Kansas City Small Business Monthly magazine and called to inquire about factoring. Shortly thereafter I met the two of them, and immediately felt comfortable with the transaction. Fess, the father, had the janitorial contacts and experience, while Les was responsible for the financial aspects of the company. They both were great people and knew their business well.

The company provided monthly cleaning services to commercial buildings. They had good accounts and billed their customers on the 25th of each month for the services provided that month. The typical turnaround time for invoice payment was 30 - 45 days. I factored all of their accounts for two years without any problem.

After the second year, Les left the business for a steady job with a guaranteed paycheck. As a small business owner, he sometimes had to skip his paycheck to cover his employee's payroll and other operational expenses. Les needed more, and found he simply couldn't live with...well, less. Fess continued with the business and his wife, Tess, took over the bookkeeping when Les left for greener pastures.

Shortly after this personnel change, Messner Janitorial Company began to struggle covering operational expenses and payroll.

Our process was to fund the invoices on the 25th of each month. Not long after she started, Tess began to press for the advance on the 20th of each month, or the 15th of each month. We did fund her invoices early several times, and soon she began to expect early advances. She decided to start billing her clients on the first of each month before the work was completed. She rationalized the "pre-billing" because their clients took 30-45 day to pay the invoice. Several clients disputed the pre-billing and stated they would not submit the invoice to accounts payable for payment until month end regardless of when the invoice was received.

I could see the company was not doing well. I continued to be concerned about the factoring relationship. The final straw occurred when Tess called requesting a wire of her rebates because she needed to put gas in the vans. She explained that her employees could not work the evening shift if we did not send the rebates immediately.

I was concerned the Messner business was not being run cleanly or efficiently and therefore decided to terminate the factoring relationship. I notified Tess of the termination and began to collect on all open invoices. I had a real concern that the company would go bankrupt and/or not be able to complete the work for invoices that were already billed and factored earlier in the month. Thankfully, we did collect on all invoices eventually.

Terminating the relationship was a hard decision because I genuinely felt sorry for the Messners. I don't believe they were bad people – just bad business owners. Fess and Tess didn't have the business savvy to run a company well and made some bad management decisions.

Four examples of their poor management included:

1. Hiring their grandchildren (Bess, Jess, Wes, and Dalrymple) as employees and overpaying them on a regular basis.

2. Not prioritizing monthly bills.

3. Not paying their vendors on a timely basis.

4. A significant payroll tax liability.

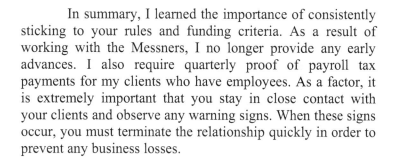

In summary, I learned the importance of consistently sticking to your rules and funding criteria. As a result of working with the Messners, I no longer provide any early advances. I also require quarterly proof of payroll tax payments for my clients who have employees. As a factor, it is extremely important that you stay in close contact with your clients and observe any warning signs. When these signs occur, you must terminate the relationship quickly in order to prevent any business losses.

Comment

This case study is a good example of the factor recognizing red flags and acting promptly, rather than just continuing to fund because the client had been with her for two years.

Even though this had been a good client, as soon as Tess took over the books she:

- Immediately began to demand earlier advances before the work was done.
- Started pre-billing her customers before the work was even started.
- Demanded rebates be wired immediately just to put gas in the trucks to do the daily work.

Compounding the problem, Tess

- Hired and regularly overpaid her grandchildren – which explains the three demands above, plus:
- Didn't prioritize monthly bills (Bess, Jess, Wes, and Dalrymple were apparently her priorities).
- Didn't pay vendors on time.
- Let a serious payroll tax liability develop.

Kim was very smart to recognize the risks she faced when Tess took over the books and the company quickly started going downhill. Pulling the plug when she did was the right move; if she had delayed like I did with Dunfore Day Care, this client, (and Kim's money) without a doubt would have turned out the same way – done for.

11.
Budibuddy Metal Fabrication

Ryan Jackiewicz
12five Capital

Lem Ecollum, owner of Budibuddy Metal Fabrication, was referred to us by a broker, Hector D. Tekter, who had a long-time relationship with our main sales contact. Hector was working as a consultant for Budibuddy in a few different areas and when the need for working capital was brought up, he immediately came to us with the prospect.

Having submitted a factoring package to us before, the document package came through nicely with all the necessary documentation. (In many instances this is often not the case.) At the time, it seemed Lem and Hector had done a good job of getting their ducks in a row and put together a complete package in order to expedite the process. As with most clients, time was of the essence, as Lem was requesting funding immediately. Since we often see this with prospects, it didn't immediately throw up a red flag.

The reason Lem wanted to factor was to improve cash flow to run the operation. Accounts receivable were turning very slowly which hampered his ability to meet payroll. Combine that with the fact that Budibuddy was growing quickly due to new state contracts, Lem had no cash on hand to purchase new inventory or material. Thus, factoring offered an attractive option by creating the working capital needed to fund these obligations.

When Lem applied for factoring, he had roughly $800,000 in A/R, although almost $500,000 of this was ineligible due to either being over 90 days or being a contra account.[1] Red flag number one, but we will get into that a bit later. We structured the factoring rates with an 80% advance, although 5% of every advance was held back in a reserve account, until that account reached 10% of his credit facility.

We gave him a total credit facility of $300,000, though each account debtor had their own facility assigned to them based on their credit worthiness. The discount rate was 4% on each invoice for the first 30 days with no additional fees whatsoever.

All Lem had to do was take that amount off his invoices' value and he could understand his true cost of funds. Rebates were structured to be released as requested by Lem, as long as he requested funds by the deadline that day. Otherwise, rebate funds were released with any advances that went out.

Budibuddy Metal Fabrication stands out due to the nature in which the deal went from seemingly good, to terrible, to finally ending with the best possible outcome.

There were many ups and downs to this deal from the get go. As stated before, Lem needed to be funded right away, though we did not let this impede us from taking every step we needed to perform the proper due diligence we felt necessary. Underwriting searches came back clean, except for a UCC filing that was on record. This was quickly terminated as there was never any funding associated between the client

---

[1] A contra account is a company to whom a client sells and also from whom it buys. An easy way to see these is by looking at AR and AP and seeing the same names. We always consider those receivables ineligible. Sometimes we consider accounts contra if the owner of our client's company is also owner of an account debtor's company.

and UCC filer. We made sure to send and confirm that all Notices of Assignment were confirmed prior to funding.

 Most important, we made sure to get written verifications for every invoice prior to funding. In most instances, a phone call verification was made to accompany the written verification. This would prove extremely important as we began to collect these invoice payments.

We funded Budibuddy roughly $300,000 over the course of two weeks in the initial funding period. Over the next 30 - 60 days, several invoices paid and we factored additional invoices, never budging from our need to receive written verification prior to funding. However, a group of invoices were aging together and not being paid. Since this was a pseudo-construction deal, the terms of the invoice varied, but were generally around 60 days. This caused us not to follow our normal aging protocol, but instead we let the invoices age a bit longer before we followed up directly.

As with most clients, Lem Ecollum requested we allow him the opportunity to try to collect before we went directly to the account debtor to collect. I don't necessarily look at this as a major mistake. Although I think that it is important that a factoring company have collection protocol in place, there is room for the client to perform some of this work for you. Not only do they save you some of the time and effort, but often they can get a quicker outcome than can the factoring company. That said, a "tight leash" should be kept on this sort of relationship where the client understands that as soon as the factoring company is not happy with the collection process, the factor will begin collection in earnest.

Back to the story. When things turned south they turned south quickly, but we didn't realize it until later. We allowed Lem to lead collection efforts longer than we should have. He kept telling us, "Don't worry, I am working on it. They are going to pay, you just have to give me time." First we were promised the account debtor would pay in one week. That turned into three weeks, and three weeks turned to six weeks. Before we knew it the invoices were outstanding for almost 100 days. This is an example of our not following established protocol for our company.

At this point, we obviously had begun the process of collecting through our own efforts. Some of this was fruitful which gave us hope we were on the right track. We collected a couple of the outstanding receivables in no time. Lem wasn't happy we were moving on without him, but this was the only plan of action we felt we could take. We pride ourselves in being client-centric, but there is always a time when the client takes advantage of that and the factoring company needs to take control.

As we continued our own collection efforts we noticed a disturbing trend. First, communication with account debtors was becoming more and more difficult by phone or email. Previously, we had no issues with this. Second, once we did reach the debtors, they all began to sing the same tune. Most had indicated they received only a portion of the product they ordered and for which they were billed. As mentioned earlier, we received written verifications for every invoice. When asked why they signed it if they hadn't received the goods, they replied "Lem called us and asked us to sign, saying when we did he would finish the order." Of course this is fraud, though we aren't sure the client understood his actions this way. This is important to remember in factoring because the act of fraud can be very blurry in the eyes of a client.

At this point, we knew we had a decent sized issue on our hands and had to escalate it to another level. We immediately called our attorney, Whitney Whitefang from The Law Office of Whitefang and Gnash, and asked her to begin whatever she thought would be necessary in this case. Since our verifications were so strong, she said we should begin with strong demand letters from her firm, hoping that the law firm letterhead would clearly show the seriousness of our position. This effort yielded some decent initial responses in the form of cash payments and settlements with debtors.

It also clued us into more details behind the relationship of Budibuddy and his debtors. Some were a little too close for comfort, as is often the case in business. In hindsight, it is not something we could have figured out ahead of time, but something that we will now try to investigate more thoroughly in the future.

Finally, we came to the point where we were still owed money but not getting positive responses from the remaining debtors. Lem had also become more difficult to work with and we decided (following Whitney's advice) to bring suit against Budibuddy and the remaining debtors. While this is obviously an expensive option, it was the right one to make at the time. The suits were filed and that is when we began to see some real action. Lem realized how serious we were and began efforts to get us paid. The debtors also looked to their own counsel, as well as Lem's, to try to get this settled.

Roughly three weeks after the suit was filed, and one week before we needed to appear in court, Lem called saying he had found money for a payoff. We gave him the payoff figure, which included principal, accrued discounts, attorney's fees, and termination fees. In the end, we received

a wire that paid off those entire amounts, except for taking a small haircut on the termination fees.

This ended in the best possible fashion, though with a great deal of headache and stress. If I learned one thing from the process, it would be to engage counsel sooner. My first inclination is to not hire an attorney, as it is usually quite costly as it was in the case. However, if it were not for the efforts of Whitefang and Gnash, we may still be trying to collect that amount. What we paid was well worth the cost.

Comment

As we saw in Case Study 4, Shifty Shuffles Staffing Services, when a client has control over the factor's contact with debtors, a problem can quickly develop – especially when that client is already defrauding you and you don't know it. In this case, Ryan followed a practice that many factors use just to save some time: he let the client make follow up calls on slow paying debtors.

In this case, Lem was far too chummy with his customers, who were way too willing to lie on the written verifications when Lem asked them. By letting Lem follow up, Ryan waited a lot longer to realize how serious his problem actually was. Fortunately, Ryan wisely took this privilege away from Lem and made the calls himself. Clearly Ryan should have done follow up himself from the start, especially in light of the dollar amount involved.

Ryan was wise to turn to his attorney right away, who handled the situation admirably. He was also lucky that the attorneys for Lem and his customers recognized their culpability, and rather than try to fight the impending lawsuit, moved quickly to settle.

Not all factors are so lucky dealing with attorneys, as we saw in Case Study 5 (Hardluck Harvey's Homes), Case Study 7 (Smallfrey Alarm Company), and as we will see in Case Study 26, Mr. Scumbucket Janitorial Company.

In short, Ryan was extremely fortunate to get his money back, with nothing more than a small pruning of his termination fees – and therefore no out of pocket losses at all. Even his attorney costs were covered. Too often, that's just the tip of the iceberg of expenses (and write offs) when lawyers get involved.

12.
Stalwart Security

Jeff Callender
Dash Point Financial

Stalwart Security is a security guard company referred by a broker. The company provides patrol guards during off hours to large construction sites and big companies who store products or equipment on outside lots, such as a roofing materials manufacturer and a large trucking company. They also provide service to a large real estate company managing a closed manufacturing plant while ownership determines what to do with the property.

The owner, Stewart Stalwart, began factoring several years ago because he needed to meet twice monthly payroll, yet his customers paid in 30 – 45 days. His volume was under $10,000 to start but he quickly grew to $30 - 40,000 and became one of my best clients. During the recession starting in 2008 his business constricted considerably and for quite some time his volume shrank to what it was when he started, but he continued factoring and has been very steady throughout his time with me.

I have charged him the same as nearly all my other clients, 1.67% every 10 days or 1% every 7 days, with an 80% advance and escrow reserve account capping at 10% of his credit line. 5% deductions are made from his advances until the cap is reached, though he has rarely needed the reserve because he has such good paying customers.

Stalwart Security is one of those clients who is a model of the kind of client you look for and want to keep for a long time – and for that matter, clone. Stewart is a calm, pleasant guy, very honest, and his large customers pay like clockwork. He always gives a heads-up when he has a new customer he wants me to check before he begins work for them.

He submits his invoices and schedules on time and is never frantic to get an advance because he is organized and uses factoring systematically and routinely. He is on time with his submissions and paperwork is always complete. In all the years he's been a client, he has never once submitted an invoice prior to work being done, for the wrong amount, or that has been disputed by customers. Notices of Assignment are accepted without incident by debtors and their payments come to our lockbox without fail.

Stalwart Security is the kind of client, especially when his volume was larger, other factors covet. In fact, Stewart told me other larger factors have contacted him hoping to lure him away from factoring with Dash Point Financial, offering lower rates and higher advances. Fortunately he has told them he is happy here and has no desire to change. In fact, he was smart enough to look closely at their "lower" rates and found all the other factors had term contracts, monthly minimums, and/or hidden fees that made factoring with them cost the same, or actually more, than what he was receiving from Dash Point.

If all accounts were as smooth and low-maintenance as this one, running a factoring business would be a piece of cake. Stewart is the perfect example of what you hope every client will be.

Comment

Did you notice all the ✛ icons in the margins of this case study? As you can tell this is an account I value very highly even though his volume has varied quite a bit over the years.

Stewart is the kind of client you want to have in your portfolio. He:

- Is honest.
- Is organized.
- Submits thorough paperwork on time.
- Is never frantic for money.
- Uses factoring properly.
- Factors consistently and steadily.
- Never has billing errors or disputes.
- Has excellent customers who:
    - Accept our NOAs without incident.
    - Always pay on time.
    - Always send their payments to our lockbox.
- Has been a client for years.
- Recognizes value of my services.
- Is very loyal.

How can you not appreciate and treasure a client like this? And the fact that he has turned away other factors courting his business is just one more feather in his cap, as far as I'm concerned.

I'll take a dozen Stewart Stalwarts! Who wouldn't?

13.

Misfit Publishing Company

Melissa Donald
LDI Growth Partners

I was introduced to Misfit Publishing Company, owned by Greg and Greta Goodfellow, by a business banker. (The manager of one of the branches he served happened to be the mother of one of my employees from a previous career.) Misfit Publishing was a small local company that needed help.

My initial observations from our first meeting were:

1) what a great guy Greg was
2) what a fun business
3) Greg and Greta were passionate about their business
4) I'm not quite sure how this would work with a factoring product.

Let's look at #4. The account debtor, Big Volume Wholesale, was a large national book distributor. Big Volume warehoused the books and shipped them to bookstores and large retailers as orders came in. On a monthly basis Big Volume sent a report to Misfit Publishing of what the sales were for that month. Over the next 60 days, any returns were taken as credits against the balance due. Then the balance due was paid the following month. Average days outstanding for an "invoice" were 90-100 days.

LDI Growth Partners has positioned itself as the factor who takes on the small, eclectic deals. This deal was certainly eclectic and, given numbers 1, 2, and 3 above, we decided to figure out how to make it work.

We structured an interesting deal and provided first funding a couple months after our initial meeting. Because we weren't sure how much would actually be paid by Big Volume due to uncertain returns each month, we diluted the invoices and used a reduced advance rate. We also extended out our penalty period to 120 days (normally 90 days). Along with that, I *strongly* urged Greg and Greta to age the invoices as long as possible before submitting them to factor; we would revisit for an increased advance rate in six months. My thinking at the time was if we could get a handle on what the true returns/credits were going to be, we could sustain a higher advance rate for the client.

Things went along really well for the first few months. Big Volume Wholesale had no issue with the notification, the reports were easy to read and understand, the dollar amounts were small and each month when we received the payment, we were always able to close out the invoice. We were gathering good data to be able to talk about restructuring the relationship.

Occasionally a month would go by without receiving a payment. We were still okay, as it was always made up the next month. We plodded along and didn't pay much attention to the warning bells, largely because communication was open and the money did seem to trickle in. And at no time did we have more than $15,000 at risk. The account kind of got lost in the shuffle.

And then…

The bankruptcy of Borders Bookstore hit like an earthquake. As stores closed, massive returns and huge payment deductions quickly followed like a tsunami. This was going to take a long time to clean up and turn around.

Because of the Borders debacle, zero payments arrived through most of the next twelve months. Then slowly we began receiving payments again from Big Volume. Pressing the client to repay us or taking a hard core collections attitude were pointless as both Greg and Greta had gone back to work at day jobs, had some health issues, and faced losing their house in foreclosure. Plodding through was the best course of action.

What is the lesson here?

Doing eclectic deals has given us a wide knowledge base for different industries and how they work, and we have been able to help some really fun and interesting people. Such deals are enjoyable. However, that said, if you come across #4 (is this a factoring deal?) and you are unsure how you are going to make it one, chances are it isn't a good prospect.

As factors we can only do deals that *are* factoring deals. Trying to package something as factoring when it is really something else is a recipe for disaster. In this case, we will be made whole over time and the relationship will simply cease, but if the dollars were larger or different, this could have been very ugly.

Comment

This is an example of a creative factor thinking outside the box of normal businesses to factor. Other industries without traditional invoices have a way of appearing on our doorsteps, and in the interest of serving a client and generating income for both businesses, many factors will take a look. As Melissa learned, however, not every such deal is "doable."

However, remember that this deal actually worked until the Borders debacle. While it wasn't making LDI loads of money, it was an interesting deal providing at least some income. Had the Borders bankruptcy not happened, chances are Melissa would still be factoring this client. Therefore another lesson is that outside influences can unexpectedly and immediately cause a disaster for small factoring clients, especially influences that you don't see coming. These can be anything from bankruptcy of major players in an industry served, to natural disasters affecting wide areas of land, to insolvent government entities as we saw in Case Study 9, Dunfore Day Care.

That is yet another good reason to keep your concentrations low, and avoid over-concentrations in any client, customer, and/or invoice. Fortunately for Melissa, she had only $15,000 invested in this client; so even if this account became a complete write off (which it didn't), her loss wouldn't have been catastrophic. As it is, she'll be waiting for some period of time to get her money back, but at least that's going to happen.

Unfortunately that's not the same ending for the factor in the next case study.

14.
Sloppee Properties

Jeff Callender
Dash Point Financial

Sloppee Properties, owned by Grumbel Sloppee, was referred by a very experienced broker. Grumbel was a man 28 years of age who had started his business two years prior to coming to Dash Point. The broker, Wilson Wizen of Silverhair Financial, was a gentleman who had been brokering various financial services including factoring for many years, and was quite experienced and professional in his referrals. He realized factoring would help Grumbel establish better cash flow, as his invoices typically took 30 – 45 days to pay.

This was his first referral to Dash Point Financial, and from his demeanor and knowledge of the business I could tell Wilson had both a thorough understanding of several financial products, and was quite good at what he did. He also happened to be a good friend of Grumbel's father, and had been well known to the Sloppee family since Grumbel was a baby. He was doing his best to help Grumbel keep his company healthy, both as a business consultant as well as a family friend.

Sloppee Properties provided restoration services for foreclosed homes. There are millions of these houses across the country these days, and restoring them for resell by the banks is big business. When previous owners move due to foreclosure, often these homes and their yards are in a state of neglect. Some have become run-down because the previous owners knew they were going to lose them and didn't have the money or inclination to maintain the property. Other former owners intentionally trash them in anger at their bank and leave them in pretty bad shape.

The banks hire companies to manage the property restorations, and these management companies in turn hire small companies like Sloppee Properties to go to the sites and do the cleanup. The jobs can range from simple lawn mowing and changing locks, to more time consuming damage repair, trash removal, and thorough cleaning inside and out. Invoices for such jobs usually range from quite small ($35 for a lawn mowing) to about $5,000 for extensive repairs, clean up and hauling. Dash Point has several clients in this business, and Sloppee was the second we funded. Most of his invoices ranged from $200 to $3,500.

We were acquainted with the management company that hired Grumbel to do the jobs, Housing and Land Property Restorations (HLPR), because they were the same debtor of our first client in this business. A large national firm, they had decent credit and paid their bills well. HLPR has a website for their small restoration companies to enable them to obtain assignments, upload before and after pictures required for each job, submit invoices, and receive notices of payment. We like sites like this because the information helps us track factored invoices and know when payment has been made.

Even though Grumbel was a young man, a personal background check revealed a Chapter 13 bankruptcy filing a year earlier that had been dismissed, and a pending Chapter 7 that had been filed just a month before he applied for factoring. While these were a bit unsettling both for a person his age and because they were so recent, searches for liens, judgments, and criminal records showed clear histories. Checks on his business revealed nothing derogatory for the two years he had been in operation.

We started Sloppee Properties with our regular $10,000 line and normal rates, which fit his needs nicely. He factored successfully for a few months and his business grew. He asked for a credit increase almost immediately (which we don't usually provide until the client has been with us long enough to establish a good track record), so I declined his initial request. However, about six months later Wilson called and said he needed to find another factor because Grumbel's volume with HLPR had doubled since he started factoring, and he needed a factor who would provide a larger credit limit. I was a little surprised at this since Grumbel hadn't mentioned anything after his initial request. Since the account was running smoothly without problems, I raised his line and everyone was happy.

Over the next few months, a few of his invoices began to be short paid, occasionally one wouldn't be paid at all, and a few we were told had been paid by payments for previous invoices. His escrow reserves were always enough to cover these so we weren't too concerned, but the pattern persisted. We asked Grumbel why HLPR wasn't paying these in full, and his response was always that their payables department wasn't very organized and they were constantly messing up his payments. We accepted his answer at first but it didn't take long for our doubts to grow, especially as the volume of short, unpaid and already paid invoices increased to where his escrow reserves no longer covered them.

My co-worker Anne contacted HLPR and asked about specific invoices with short or no payments. She found that for each of them, Grumbel's work was either substandard or incomplete. For one of his larger invoices, he had left the job unfinished and HLPR had to use another restoration company to complete it. Clearly they weren't happy with Grumbel's work and as a result they weren't giving him as much business as they had previously (which made Grumbel grumble even more). Further, some invoices weren't paid because he hadn't submitted photographs, showing the work was done (even though he factored them). These photos were understandably required for payment from HLPR. Again Grumbel's response was that the work had been done and the photos submitted; HLPR was just wrong and incompetent. His agitation visibly grew.

Over time, as more problem invoices emerged, Anne found Grumbel had submitted invoices for work on properties that HLPR didn't even have in their system. Obviously they weren't going to pay for work on houses for which they had no record. When she contacted Grumbel to ask about these, he didn't return her calls and cut off all contact. We worked with HLPR to be sure all payments would continue coming to Dash Point, and they were quite cooperative. We both realized Sloppee Properties was bad news, and Grumbel was a very unreliable individual who accepted no responsibility for his own mistakes. His pattern was to do shoddy work, blame someone else for it, then complain he was being victimized.

We continued to work with HLPR to get the remaining invoices paid, and when the last of the undisputed payments was received we were still out about $14,000 including discounts due ($11,000 in advances). Meanwhile I had called Wilson to ask him to contact Grumbel since our calls were not being returned and we had a problem. He was disturbed to hear this and said he would certainly contact Grumbel. However he called back a couple weeks later and said he had made numerous attempts but his calls also went unreturned.

I described Grumbel's poor paperwork and his pattern of blaming others for his own shortcomings. Wilson acknowledged this was indeed an accurate assessment. While I was glad to have my observations confirmed, I was troubled that Wilson hadn't acknowledged these character flaws until now. I was also disturbed because I knew this meant getting paid back was going to be very difficult if not impossible. What's more, Wilson also said Grumbel had started a day job and was no longer working his restoration business. There was a suggestion that his mother and sister had taken over the company but this was quite vague and we were unable to contact them or confirm that was the case. We were getting nowhere.

At this point we gave the account to our collection attorney, Cleaver Squeezem, who (like everyone else) attempted to contact Grumbel without success. He gave up the fight fairly quickly and we turned to our collection agency, Onus, Dred & Trembal. They also worked the account, trying for a short time to contact his family (who we discovered were people of some means and social standing in the community). But Onus also got nowhere and gave up.

I had my doubts from the beginning that Grumbel's parents would bail out their irresponsible son. After all, they let him declare bankruptcy (or try to) twice in the same year recently. They appear to be quite familiar with his manner of dealing with problems he creates (whimper and blame someone else), and are willing to let him live with the consequences of his irresponsibility yet again. Unfortunately, that means people and companies (like Dash Point and who knows how many more from his bankruptcy) Grumbel leaves in his wake are the ones who will continue to suffer the losses. Grumbel will just go his merry way, get another job, and not care a hoot about the people he's harmed.

I'm sure Grumbel has learned nothing from this experience and he will continue to whine and complain when his own shoddy work and immature attitude continue to contaminate everything he touches. If he ever does and become a responsible adult, I expect it will be far, far in the future and my loss will be long past.

But quite honestly, I don't really think that will ever happen.

Comment

This is the kind of client that can make you a jaded factor. Here is a man who complains, lies, and blames everyone else for the problems he creates. When you work with a client like this with the intention of trying to help his business (as have plenty of others, such as Wilson Wizen, and an attorney who briefly represented Grumbel when Onus was pressing for payment), and he does nothing but make your life miserable in the process, your patience quickly evaporates. You want such people out of your life.

Toxic people like Grumbel spread their own tinge of misery across everyone upon whom their shadow falls. All you can do is extricate yourself from the relationship as quickly and as completely as you can, and move on. Of the few people in my life with whom I have been truly sorry to have crossed paths, Grumbel Sloppee is one of them. You'll read about a couple more in later case studies.

Fortunately other clients serve as a balance to such poisonous people. The next case study describes one of them.

15.

Gogetter Property Services

Jeff Callender
Dash Point Financial

Garrett Gogetter, the owner of Gogetter Property Services in the Midwest, found Dash Point's website with a web search when he was looking for a factor. A man in his mid-30's, Garrett had purchased his company about a year and a half earlier and like many, found his business was hampered by cash flow problems caused by waiting 30 – 45 days to be paid. He learned about factoring, realized it was just what his company needed to grow, and sought a factor on his own.

He had almost no receivables when he started looking for a factor, but was convinced factoring would enable his business to be be very successful. He contacted several factors who all turned him down because his volume was so small. When he found Dash Point's website, which made clear we welcome accounts his size, he was relieved and excited to find a factor who might accept him. When I told him we had worked with other small companies in the real estate restoration industry and were familiar with how his business functions and the receivables flow, he was quite enthusiastic about working with us. He submitted his application and couldn't wait to get started; the eagerness in his voice came through loud and clear. This is just what I like to hear from a prospective client when we begin looking at an account.

He listed four customers, one for whom he was working and three for whom he was considering doing work. Underwriting them showed all were good payers and would be acceptable as debtors. Due diligence on Garrett's company showed a clear record, though his personal background revealed a personal judgment for $9400 with a bank. Fortunately, he was already on a payment program for that obligation and was making regular monthly payments. I decided to proceed and accept Garrett as a client, providing our standard advance and discount rates.

When we sent the NOA to his first customer, Unapproachable Property Management, and followed up with our usual phone call, we were informed they did not work with factors and were quite unwilling to budge an inch. While such reluctance does not legally negate the validity of the NOA, I do not buy invoices to uncooperative debtors because it means we're dealing with a company that 1) will be unhelpful if not hostile, 2) won't accept our phone calls, and 3) will continue to send payments to the client. Buying invoices to such companies creates immediate (and ongoing) problems I don't want.

I informed Garrett of Unapproachable's position and why we couldn't factor invoices to them. He was keenly disappointed but understood, and agreed we shouldn't factor customers with that attitude. What's more, he said he didn't even want to work with people like that. I liked his thinking! I suggested he contact the next customer he wanted to factor to see if we would run into a similar problem before either of us spent time or effort setting up the account. Remarkably, they wouldn't work with us either.

Garrett was getting quite discouraged by these unexpected turns, and I was quite surprised to have two consecutive negative customer attitudes. While I run across an occasional debtor who feels this way about factors, I have never had two in a row from the same client be so factor-unfriendly. I wondered if it was the industry and/or the fact that these people didn't really understand factoring. At any rate, I told Garrett that as soon as he had a customer who would work with Dash Point, we would be happy to fund him.

Quite honestly I didn't expect to hear back from him and figured this was a client we were going to lose. However, Garrett's eagerness to factor his receivables and his can-do attitude prevailed. A few weeks later he called and said he had a customer, Enlightened Property Managers, who had no problems working with us. He established an account with them and was ready to go.

Enlightened had a good credit rating. We contacted them, found they were happy to sign our NOA, and were quite ready to provide Gogetter with several jobs to get started. Garrett's enthusiasm was almost palpable and he began work immediately. Enlightened had a website that allowed Garrett and Dash Point to track his jobs and payments, and when the first payments came through just as the site indicated, we were all happy campers.

Garrett continued to factor successfully for the next few months, and his business grew as he knew it would. To our surprise, one day we received a call from Enlightened who asked if we were interested in accepting a company that was another vendor of theirs, who was also interested in factoring his receivables. This was a first for us – getting an unrequested referral from a debtor who not only recognized we were helping its vendors, but who liked our service because it made their vendors more stable. We took the referral and followed up with our new prospect.

That business appeared to fit our parameters nicely, cleared underwriting with flying colors, and since we already knew the debtor was fine, we began factoring that account as well. Since then, Enlightened Property Managers referred us three additional clients. We reached a point where our concentrations with this debtor were as far as we wanted to go, and two of these clients have turned out to be very good clients.

Wanting to continue to grow his company, Garrett asked us if we knew of any other foreclosure management companies that might accept him as a vendor. We referred him to Housing and Land Property Restorations (HLPR), the same debtor we had worked with on the Sloppee Properties account, and he immediately contacted them. They have accepted him as a vendor and he has begun work for HLPR as well, and he of course intends to factor his receivables with them.

Gogetter's account continues to grow and he remains one of our most enthusiastic clients (and fans!). He appreciates what we do for him, is very cooperative and responsive, always submits his schedules on time, and is a delight to work with. We have raised his credit limit and he will soon need another increase due to the growth his company is experiencing.

Comment

This is the kind of client factors love: an enthusiastic, eager-beaver business owner who wants to grow his company, understands and appreciates the value of factoring, uses it properly and to everyone's advantage, and soundly manages his steady (but not too rapid) growth. This account has turned into a win-win not only for Gogetter and Dash Point, but an additional win for his debtor, Enlightened Property Managers.

Referring their vendors to Dash Point has helped Enlightened's business by stabilizing the vendors they need to do their work. In that industry, such providers are often very small operations who, when they start, have few assets other than a truck and very basic equipment. These little guys badly need stable cash flow, and without it often don't last long. Having a factoring source for their vendors helps Enlightened just as much as it helps their very small, struggling vendors, and Dash Point.

16.

Audacity Cleaning Service

Tony Neglia
Stonebridge Financial Services

Audacity Cleaning Services, owned by Floyd Fibberlips, was a small cleaning company that focused on post construction cleanup. He was referred by a broker. This deal went south from the first invoice which wasn't entirely the fault of Floyd – although he quickly made it much worse.

Audacity Cleaning had one customer, Coveryerbutt Construction, with pretty good credit. The set up was fairly easy; Floyd signed and returned the contract promptly and Coveryerbutt Construction signed and returned the NOA properly. They verified (via telephone) the first invoice for $4,500 was approved for payment, and a few weeks later likewise verified the second invoice for $9,500 was also approved for payment.

Sometime later when payment for the first invoice was late, I contacted Floyd to ask if he knew anything about the status of the payment. He said he did not so I contacted the account debtor directly. They admitted they made a mistake and sent payment directly to Floyd. At this point it wasn't a big deal since there was another invoice behind it. If the customer would send us the second payment we would be made whole and everyone would be happy. Of course, I now realized Floyd lied when he told me he hadn't received payment, and had no information on its status. That being the case, the factoring relationship was over. Nevertheless, we wouldn't lose much money on the deal if we were sent payment for the second, larger, invoice for $9,500.

Unfortunately, rather than fixing their mistake, Coveryerbutt Construction lived up to their name and contacted their attorney, Conrad Clientshield, to help them figure out what they should do. At that point they refused to take my calls and directed me to contact Mr. Clientshield. Sheesh!

This was very interesting because Coveryerbutt initially admitted the mistake, but now their attorney was explaining why it wasn't a mistake and why they were obligated to send the checks to Floyd, their vendor, instead of Stonebridge. Basically, Conrad explained, since Audacity Cleaning was a sole proprietor and payments to Floyd constituted wages, those payments were not assignable. I told him I understood this legal argument but our contract's wording explicitly states the transaction was "commercial in nature, and not for household, family, consumer and/or personal use." Nevertheless, Conrad told me that despite their position he was going to contact Floyd Fibberlips and try to get him to agree to allow Coveryerbutt Construction to send payment for the second invoice to me.

Conrad did as he said and was successful. Floyd agreed to let them send payment for the second invoice to Stonebridge. As a side note, Conrad told me Floyd was concerned he would not receive his rebate if payment for the second invoice were sent to us. Do you believe the nerve?! He had diverted a payment of $4,500 and now was concerned that he wouldn't get a rebate on his second invoice.

To Conrad's credit, I believe he was acting in the best interest of his client and still managed to find a solution that kept everyone happy. However, it was interesting to see how legal maneuvering works. The account debtor messed up and their attorney tried to find legal justification for why they did what they did. Fortunately the attorney in this case saw the bigger picture, realized I had been defrauded and lied to, and attempted to make things right.

In the end, I was almost made whole (losing only a few hundred dollars) but this was another close call in the construction industry. Further, I stopped funding sole proprietors for nearly a year. I have since reversed this policy but am very aware of the legal pitfalls. I try to keep deals with sole proprietors small in case similar situations arise in the future.

Comment

The gall of some clients is really hard to believe; Floyd Fibberlips is a perfect example. Here is a man who, with his very first factored invoice, told a bald-faced lie to Tony when asked if he knew what had happened to the payment. He said he didn't know, but had actually received and cashed the check! Incredible.

Then, even harder to believe, when Tony received payment for the second check, he had the cheek to say he wanted his rebate for that check! Did he think Tony didn't know what he had done? Or wouldn't care? Some people not only have incredible nerve, they are complete idiots when dealing with people and have totally unrealistic expectations.

The bright spot in this case study, surprisingly, is Floyd's attorney, Conrad Clientshield. While he started off playing the role of protecting his client at the expense of all other parties, Conrad recognized the dishonesty of his client's vendor. He realized Tony was truly wronged by him, and had the decency to try to make things right. To his credit, he did.

After dealing with the likes of unpleasant attorneys from other case studies (Neville Knozsquatt, Stickittooem & Bulleys, and later D'Lay, Obstrukt & Hindir), as well as dishonest clients like Floyd Fibberlips and others (Jay Blahzay, Dee Seetful, Willie B. Wiley, Harvey Hoodwinker, Lem Ecollum, and more to come), working with a decent

person like Conrad gives one hope for humanity. I mean –
he's an *attorney* who actually did the right thing.

17.
Lunch & Munch Staffing

Kim Deveney
American Funding Solutions

One of my best clients is Lunch & Munch Staffing, owned by Candi Cotten, which provides workers for large events. This client was referred by another factoring company which required a monthly minimum. Candi didn't feel comfortable committing to a monthly minimum because her business is seasonal.

Lunch & Munch Staffing provides staff to work concession stands at local sporting events (usually for a major league baseball team) and concerts. Candi hires workers as subcontractors on an hourly basis for each event. She pays her staff after completion of their paperwork and adding hours worked in a pay period. After calculating hours worked by all staff, she prepares an invoice for her customer.

The Food Brood, her customer, is a large hospitality company with excellent credit. They have been in business for 75 years and are a strong debtor. Upon receiving an invoice they consistently remit payment within 15-30 days.

Four years ago, Candi starting factoring just a few invoices each month but has grown steadily each year. With factoring, she has been able to bid on larger contracts with confidence knowing she will have the working capital to cover payroll expense. She has provided over 500 staff people at certain events which would have been impossible before factoring. Her invoices are always paid within 30 days

123

which helps to keep her factoring costs low while still providing sufficient cash flow for her business.

Candi factors $10,000 to $40,000 per month depending on the season. She is extremely busy in the spring and summer with concerts and the baseball season. Her business picks up again in the fall through football season before it slows down in January and February. As a factor, this client is ideal for several reasons.

1. She hires subcontractors, not employees. Therefore we don't have to worry about payroll tax payments. Many small businesses with employees get behind in paying their payroll tax obligation. Payroll tax problems can often be the downfall of a small business.

2. Her customer is strong and pays invoices within 30 days.

3. She provides excellent communication of upcoming events and her anticipated funding needs.

4. She has detailed invoices and sign-offs for each invoice.

5. The invoices are always paid promptly and without any offsets or short payments.

In addition, Candi is one of my best advocates and regularly tells other business owners about factoring and how it has benefited her business. She is a great referral source for my business. She is a perfect example of how factoring can help a business grow and become more successful.

Comment

Like other prize clients we've seen, Lunch & Munch Staffing has many characteristics of the kind of company you look for when marketing for new business:

- Excellent communication regarding upcoming funding needs.
- Signed invoices that are clear and detailed.
- An excellent debtor who always pays promptly.

- Payments that never are short paid or include offsets (deductions for something the client owes the debtor).
- She regularly "beats the drum" for factoring in general and Kim in particular.

What more can you ask for? As Kim put it so well, Lunch and Munch Staffing is "a perfect example of how factoring can help a business grow and become successful." After all, that's why we're factors in the first place, right?

18.

Dorrie Nobb Advertising

Tony Neglia
Stonebridge Financial Services

Dorrie Nobb Advertising was a referral from a fellow factor who noticed the prospect was practically a neighbor of mine and was kind enough to pass it along to us. It was also a start-up business. Owner Dorrie Nobb provided print advertising for local businesses. He would go through residential neighborhoods hanging plastic bags filled with buckslip ads (inserts about the size of a dollar bill) from local businesses on front doors.

I thought this was an interesting business and welcomed the opportunity to work with a local client (most of my clients are located more than 100 miles away). The invoices were fairly small ($200-$400 per month) and since the business was new with just a few customers, there wasn't much risk. All the account debtors were notified properly; we require the account debtors to sign the assignment letters and fax them back to us so we know they have made the appropriate changes to their accounts payable system.

Although small, this account was initially going well. Dorrie then decided to factor invoices for products he was selling on eBay. While this wasn't his core business, we felt comfortable with it after we saw how invoices could be verified on eBay's invoicing system.

I believe it was the eBay experience that derailed Dorrie. Payments from eBay very often did not materialize. We never figured out if Dorrie did not deliver the product, delivered a defective product, or (as he claimed) eBay was just being difficult and withholding payments unnecessarily.

While this aspect of his business was not working out, Dorrie was adding additional advertising customers. This was about the time he asked us not to verify every invoice because his business customers did not like getting calls from us. This was a major red flag! Nevertheless, I agreed but under the stipulation that if some of the late payments didn't come in quickly, all funding would cease. Naturally, payments did not come in and all funding ceased. Additionally, Dorrie stopped returning our phone calls and emails.

We have found this is a common occurrence when a client has his back to the wall. The debt was only about $4,000 - $5,000 and we probably would have settled for much less than that if he had been willing to negotiate in good faith with us (we require personal guarantees on every deal). However, Dorrie would not contact us.

Since he was local we decided to sue him and his business. A local friend (attorney) agreed to represent Stonebridge. After he was served, Dorrie decided to contact me. He explained he was going to sue me because I ruined his business when I decided to cease funding. Our contract explicitly states that we are not required to purchase invoices at any time so this was a nonstarter – we pointed out this clause to him.

Next he told me he would declare bankruptcy if I won. We have found this is a common refrain the few times we have had to threaten legal action. Later he sent a letter explaining he owed the IRS about $70,000 and they would get paid before Stonebridge, so he considered himself "judgment proof." Upon informing us of his IRS debt, I thanked him for documenting his fraud: his application stated that he did not owe any back taxes and our background search did not find anything (or he was lying about IRS) and gave the letter to my attorney.

At the first court date Dorrie showed up without an attorney and asked for a continuance which the judge granted. At this point he realized we were serious. The new court date was 60 days later. On the 59th day he called and asked if we would settle. We agreed but at this point the debt (discounts, penalties, attorney costs, etc.) had ballooned to $13,000. Further, he did not have any cash – or so he claimed.

We agreed that if he paid us $9,000 ($500 up front plus $300 per month) that we would forgive the remainder. However, a judgment would be issued for $13,000 and if he were ever late with any payment we would hold him responsible for the full $13,000. To this day we are receiving monthly checks for $300; not one has been missed.

I have thought a lot about this case and I do not believe Dorrie set out to defraud me. I have concluded that he just got himself in a bind and couldn't find a way out. Rather than confront his problem head on he ran away, as this is what he concluded was in his best interest. In the end he is paying much more than he would have if he worked with us when things initially went wrong.

Comment

This is the age-old lesson of life, as well as factoring: when you have a problem, confront it and deal with it directly; don't run away and try to hide. That only makes things worse.

A great many factoring losses and fraud start like this did: the client simply wanted to factor to improve his business. He did nothing wrong at first, but soon find himself in a bind when eBay didn't pay as expected. As Tony said, "it was the eBay experience that derailed Dorrie."

This is why you must impress on new clients which customers they should factor, and which they should not. They should factor only those whom they are confident will pay in a timely fashion, and in full. If customers pay late, partially, or erratically, both the client and factor end up regretting factoring them. Dorrie is the perfect example of why. From the factor's side, be as sure as sure as you can that the invoices you buy are to good-paying debtors with no issues... or this is the kind of thing that can result.

Tony is fortunate that Dorrie has honored his workout agreement. In many cases (such as we'll see in Case Study 26, Mr. Scumbucket Janitorial Company) when clients get into a hole and small regular payments are the only way to pay back the factor, too often these payments are made for a time and then just fade away. Tony's agreement has very sharp teeth to enforce this workout: if Dorrie is ever late the full judgment amount will be required. Hopefully that will keep Dorrie's feet to the fire until the amount he owes is fully paid.

19.

Clank Brothers Wiring and Cable

Melissa Donald
LDI Growth Partners

Clank Brothers Wiring and Cable was a corporation owned and operated by brothers Tiff and Wrangle Clank. They specialized in wiring and cabling installation at hospitals. Their largest account debtor was a strong regional hospital in the middle of a huge expansion and retrofitting project. They were referred by a banker I met at a local Chamber of Commerce breakfast where I was the featured speaker.

My company quickly established a good relationship with the AP department contact and fell into a rhythm of sending her a spreadsheet of invoices submitted to us for verification. She was very timely in response. Over the next 6-8 months, we would occasionally advance before we got her response, but there was rarely any issue...maybe the occasional missed invoice that we would send over. Payments were made to us without any issue every week, paying invoices between 40-45 days old. It was a beautiful thing.

After about a year, we realized Tiff and Wrangle were not getting along and they were putting me in the middle of their drama. They decided to go their separate ways. I had a much better relationship with Wrangle and his wife Jean, and it was Wrangle who was going to be taking the major accounts and going off on his own. He needed our help.

Given the history of the relationship and how amazingly well it had gone, we jumped right in with some additional funding to cover Wrangle's startup costs. He was up and running in a few months and began factoring immediately.

When he ventured out on his own and changed the name of the company, his AP rep at the major account changed to a new individual, Rosa Thorne. We were never able to build a good relationship with her. We still thought we were okay because we had such good history.

Unfortunately, things slowly began to erode. After a time we would have a chunk of invoices that were really old; when we would question it, Rosa would say she did not have the invoices and then Wrangle would buy them back. There was also an increased sense of urgency about every funding. The requests would come in later and later, followed by frantic emails and calls asking us to push things though. Almost without fail, we accommodated Wrangle and Jean. This went on for a while and then I called for a sit down meeting.

In that meeting there were a lot of excuses, but the bottom line was we were getting invoices that were being generated from proposals for work not yet started, let alone completed.

We thought we had to do whatever we had to do to salvage the relationship because

1) We could not wrap our heads around these particular people doing bad stuff.

2) The client had become the largest source of revenue we had.

3) If we stopped funding, we ran the risk of not getting our money back because we still were not entirely sure

which items on the aging were bona fide invoices and which were just proposals for work not even started. It was terrifying for us.

By now the economy had thrown the world into a tailspin and our investors were taking a closer interest in what we were doing. We worked with them to establish new funding guidelines and told our clients the new rules. To say it was met with resistance is an understatement.

We limped along with this client until the end of the year. During the week between Christmas and New Years, they were over their limit, our concentration with them was way out of whack, we had about $100K in "fake" invoices on the books, and the weekly payment from the account debtor had not arrived. We drew an immoveable line in the sand and said we would not fund anything more until the weekly payment arrived, which we knew would be close to $100K. We had copies of remittance reports and copies of checks from the hospital. We were checking our mailbox several times a day.

It was intense and ugly and there was a lot of screaming and cussing (at me, not by me). In the first couple of days of January, Wrangle was begging us to fund him based on the remit reports from the hospital, telling us the checks must have been lost in the mail due to the holidays. We held our ground and did not fund. A couple of days later, Wrangle told me that he had deposited the checks into his account – a little over $95K. Incredibly, the checks were made out to LDI Growth Partners – not him. It was after he deposited the checks that he asked us to fund based on the remit reports.

In May we initiated a lawsuit against the bank for allowing the checks to be deposited. They still have not returned our money to us and we are set for trial in the summer. To date they have forced us to spend over half the amount of the claim to litigate. Wrangle gave away his business and he and Jean filed bankruptcy. We have sued them in the bankruptcy for non-dischargeability because of the fraud he committed. Occasionally Wrangle still contacts me with some new idea for how he is going to pay us back...if only we would give him a little money to get restarted and stop all this pesky litigation. We will stay the course.

What are the lessons here?

1. First and foremost, create policies and procedures with which you are comfortable and then do not deviate from them. If you do (and come on, we all do), be sure you effectively communicate this is an *exception* to an established rule.

2. Don't ever get too comfortable with the paper or the people. That doesn't mean that you should act like the money police necessarily, but it is wise to always trust but verify. In this case, this client became a "friend." It was because of that "friendship" that I told my little voice to hush, that everything would be fine.

3. The most important lesson is to **never** hush that little voice. If your little voice is throwing a temper tantrum, *listen to it*. Even if you aren't exactly sure what it is trying to tell you, listen to the fact that it is present. Do not let a client's or broker's urgency make you second guess yourself when funding. If your hand starts to shake as it hovers over the send button, don't press the send button.

Comment

Like most, this case study started well and the account cruised along for some time. But when storm clouds gathered (in this instance, when Tiff and Wrangle started...well, their tiffs and wrangling), things never improved. Their good contact at the debtor's company changed to Rosa Thorne who was of no help, invoices didn't pay properly and were getting charged back, and soon Wrangle started getting impatient and nasty when he needed funds.

Melissa graciously accommodated his demands to "push things through" for a while, but as a factor this cannot be sustained. Factors can only buy good invoices for work completed – not invoices "being generated from proposals for work not yet started, let alone completed." Submitting such "invoices" (which is fraud) and funding them (which should never be done) is the kiss of death for a factoring relationship.

Doing so put both LDI and Wrangle in a very difficult spot. Melissa did this because at first she couldn't bring herself to believe that Wrangle had been defrauding her this way (though he had). Further, this account provided more income for LDI than any other, and to stop funding could lead to a quick and very serious loss of both income and operating capital.

The crowning blow was when Wrangle escalated his demands (despite his dishonesty) with "screaming and cussing," and then had the gall to cash a check made out to LDI – and *still* demanded she fund him further. This is a sign of a truly desperate client that spells nothing but trouble, and from whom you need to exit as soon as possible, no matter how much you make from them or how much capital is invested in them.

Fortunately Melissa took the right steps after this blew up – suing the bank for improperly cashing the check for Wrangle, and then suing his bankruptcy proceedings (no big surprise he made that move) for "non-dischargeability because of the fraud he committed." There's really not much more LDI can do in this instance and considering the costs already incurred in the lawsuit against the bank, this can only end in a sizeable write off. If she's lucky, some money might be recouped from the bank, but odds are not in her favor she'll get much else.

The regular reappearance of Wrangle trying to obtain more funds from Melissa is somewhat incredible, though actually not that unusual. When clients have received funds from a factor they've fooled before, they somehow think that coming up with new schemes to generate income is going to be welcomed by the factor. How wrong they are. I have had (former) clients do this with me as well, and all I want from them is to just go away.

This case study has some hard-learned lessons for Melissa, and readers do well to take note and heed her advice. First, follow your own rules. Second, listen to that "little voice" that is telling you something. When you don't do either, this is what can happen.

20.

Hemisphere and World Loagistics International Transfer (HAWLIT)

Rodrigo Riadi
Front Range Factoring

Hemisphere and World Logistics International Transfer (HAWLIT), a container drayage trucking company, was referred by another factor. The company's owner, Clyde Dale, showed several reasons not to factor him prior to funding, and required extra due diligence to create his account. Fortunately in the end Clyde became a very good client.

What is container drayage? Drayage originally referred to transporting products by a cart. These carts, pulled by large, strong horses called dray or draft horses, were used to move goods from ships or railroad cars to factories, warehouses and shops. We see a vestige of the practice nowadays in Budweiser commercials with the big horses pulling a large red wagon full of cases of beer.

Today drayage refers to the transport of shipping containers by specialized trucking companies between ocean ports or rail ramps to shipping docks. A container is moved from a port or rail yard to another location, such as a logistics depot distribution center. Once unloaded, the truck returns to the initial pick-up point.

HAWLIT worked at a major U.S. port for a handful of customers, and wanted to factor a single customer who paid once per month. The customer, Goodsnstuff International, was based outside the U.S. Although a U.S. branch company existed, all trade payables were paid via wire transfer from headquarters abroad.

Goodsnstuff International was publicly traded abroad, and my initial investigations revealed good credit. Given the foreign nature of the company, however, obtaining trade credit information added some time and expense to the process. Further, no contract between HAWLIT and GI existed; however, a multi-year relationship existed between the two.

As I started underwriting, I found several companies with names very similar to HAWLIT existed, which were close to or at the same location, and the names of most owners were not Clyde Dale. Some owners had large tax liens and other potential issues in their background; Clyde had a few minor judgments against him but nothing more. One of the companies (not Clyde's) had an outstanding UCC from a factoring company; unfortunately that factoring company did not return my calls.

When performing due diligence on a new factoring prospect, it is often easier to look for reasons not to fund, and HAWLIT Trucking provided several:

1. He had a foreign debtor; this alone can kill a deal. Obtaining trade credit information for foreign debtors can be expensive and the information obtained may be of uncertain reliability. Further, collecting from foreign accounts may not be viable.

2. The corporate entity of the company and who owned it were unclear. This raised a few red flags as it is one way diversion of funds can take place as well as a potential attempt to hide past issues. The fact that another factor was involved at some point indicated

this might be a possibility. Further, the one owner with a questionable background added to the potential risk of moving forward without further due diligence and clarification.

3. No contract was in place between HAWLIT and Goodsnstuff, although this is not a deal killer with a domestic debtor. But the lack of contract compounds the risk of dealing with a foreign debtor by not providing documented terms upon which the services of the prospect are provided, or payments made. This could also further complicate any collection efforts. Separately, the lack of a contract compounded the fuzzy identity of the prospect, a very significant issue.

To address the matter of his company name and ownership I contacted Clyde and asked for clarification. He explained he had worked for a company with a similar name for several years during which he learned the business. He had just purchased the assets and customer relationship from the old company, a transaction I was able to confirm. Clyde had chosen a similar name to avoid disturbing the relationship with his customer. The old company owner had factored his receivables but was not satisfied with the service, so he recommended Clyde find another factor. The scenario described seemed plausible so I decided to proceed with caution.

I obtained reliable credit information for the Goodsnstuff International abroad; however, credit information for the U.S. sub was almost non-existent. The debtor's credit abroad turned out to be very good so I again decided to proceed with caution.

Wanting to contact the debtor directly, I made the prospect a proposal which was accepted after some haggling. I drafted a contract and, once signed, notified the debtor and attempted to establish communication to address my concerns. After some back and forth, I was able to establish good rapport with the debtor and understand its relationship with HAWLIT, which confirmed what Clyde told me.

During this process and to help the debtor recognize us as their supplier's payee, we helped Clyde communicate to Goodsnstuff there had been a change in ownership, but otherwise everything would remain the same. Clyde was hesitant to have this conversation with his customer, fearing for the integrity of the relationship. Our intervention helped establish him as the vendor and us as the factor in the debtor's eyes. From my perspective, this intervention satisfactorily mitigated my risk in this transaction.

On the other hand, during conversations with Goodsnstuff it also became clear full invoice verification would not be possible as the debtor for one reason or another could not confirm the services were provided. In many situations this alone would be a deal killer. In this case and at 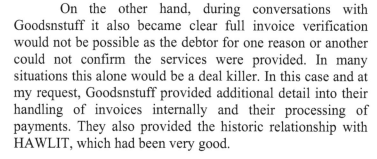 my request, Goodsnstuff provided additional detail into their handling of invoices internally and their processing of payments. They also provided the historic relationship with HAWLIT, which had been very good.

After evaluating all the information available I decided to fund the account. Clyde went on to become an excellent client for about a year, after which he no longer needed my service. I never had any issues with him other than occasional minor billing mistakes.

Despite mitigating some of the risks involved in this case, I could not fully reduce the risks to the level with which I am typically comfortable, particularly due to the verification issue that came up late in the underwriting process. At some point I had to make a decision as to whether the risks were worth taking given the available information. I decided to move forward and, in this case, the results favored that decision.

Comment

Rodrigo took several risks funding this client. Clyde "showed several reasons not to factor him prior to funding":

- His corporate status was muddy.
- He had a foreign debtor.
- He didn't have a contract with the foreign debtor.
- The debtor couldn't confirm services had been provided, so the invoices couldn't be verified.

Any of these points alone would be reason for many factors to decline this prospect, and most would probably turn this prospect away given the risks and warning signs involved. However, after weighing all the pros and cons, Rodrigo decided to fund anyway.

He was quite lucky this turned out to be a good client. As we see in so many of these case studies, that doesn't always end up being the case. Clyde Dale is an example of the fact that you simply *never* know which new clients will be good experiences, and which will be bad.

Therefore you need to keep up your guard for every account you have, new and long-standing. With every client you need to do exactly what Rodrigo did here: "proceed with caution."

21.
Techie Trekker

Jeff Callender
Dash Point Financial

Techie Trekker, owned by Jacob Jobber, is a one-person computer programming company. Jacob has high-level programming skills and works as an independent contractor on projects for one company at a time. Typically these jobs are full-time placements that last between a few months to about a year. When a project is completed, just as his company name suggests, he moves on to the next one with a new company.

While he is well paid for what he does, Jacob's living expenses and personal financial responsibilities are such that he can't meet them without factoring, since most of his placements pay him about a month after the current month's work is completed. He tried to manage before he heard about factoring and had a rough time doing so. When he learned of factoring about five years ago, he immediately recognized it would solve his cash flow problems and quickly began looking for a factor. Searching the internet, Jacob found several larger factors who all said his volume was too small to meet their requirements. After further searching he found Dash Point and realized we were a good fit.

While each company he works for has somewhat different payment practices, the ones he factors wait 15 - 30 days after a month's work is completed before paying. Because of personal weekly expenses he is obligated to pay, he can't afford to wait that long to receive his check. Thus Jacob factors each week for the work he's just completed. The time elapsed from the time Dash Point gives weekly advances, to the time we receive a monthly payment, ranges from three to eight weeks. His customers are creditworthy and he has me check out each one before signing a contract. In most cases assigning his payments to Dash Point is not an issue with the debtor.

I charge him my standard rates and his invoices, depending on the project, are around $2,000 - $3,000 per week. Thus his monthly volume is in the $8,000 to $12,000 range. Since he is usually paid monthly about 15 to 30 days after month end, my exposure ranges between $4,000 to $18,000.

If a company pays him early enough that he doesn't need to factor, I don't hear from him for several months while he's on that project. However, when it ends and the next one is going to pay less promptly, he calls right away to have me run credit on the new company, re-activate his account, and put the NOA in place. He likes having everything completely prepared and ready to go before he begins the first day of work on a new project.

Jacob is a somewhat intense person and becomes quite agitated when his customer doesn't pay when expected. He is also quite conscious of his factoring costs. When his customer pays later than they're supposed to he knows full well their tardiness is costing him money – which irritates him no end. He has no problem going into the office of the CEO and letting him know if he's not being paid when the contract states he should be. Thus he provides excellent follow up if a payment is late and because he watches his aging reports like a hawk, we never have to tell him when a payment is past due. He already knows and has taken steps to resolve it.

Jacob keeps us on our toes to make sure he gets his weekly advances on time; if we slip up he lets us know right away. But his volume is an amount I like, his customer payments are usually dependable, and if they're late he is all over them like white on snow. This makes his account one of my favorites and despite his somewhat gruff demeanor, I really like working with him.

Comment

Here is another example of a client of whom you'd like a dozen more. While Jacob is a bit grumpy at times, he is extremely organized, always on time with his paperwork, has good steady and very consistent volume with good paying customers, and collecting from a slow payer is never a problem.

I miss his account when he's working on an unfactored project, but he always comes back when he needs our service. He appreciates factoring and how it makes his life much easier, and has made it clear he couldn't meet his obligations without it. I expect he'll be a client whenever he has a project that won't pay immediately (which is most of them) and he'll by in our portfolio for a long time to come.

Just what every factor wants!

22.

Smuggley, Swindol & Finkbottom Finance

Don D'Ambrosio
Oxygen Funding

Oxygen Funding works with hundreds of brokers who bring us prospects to evaluate and ultimately fund their invoices. To be a broker with Oxygen we provide a formal, signed Broker Agreement that spells out legal terms including compensation to a referring broker on deals we fund. This case study shows both brokers and smaller factors how important having such a written contract is when referring any deal to a funder – and having it signed *before* the prospect is introduced.

One of our brokers, D.L. Phinder, referred a prospect named Buymyhy Tech Products who imported electronics from Asia and then sold them to high end retail chain stores in the United States. Buymyhy's business was expanding quickly and generating approximately $2,000,000 a month in invoices, with the expectation of doubling that amount in the next three months.

Buymyhy's volume was above our maximum credit limit for a single client so we quickly informed D.L. we would not be in a position to fund the prospect ourselves. Since this prospect involved several million dollars in monthly invoices, D.L. asked if we would be interested in co-brokering the deal if we could help him find a funding source. We agreed on an appropriate commission split and proceeded to send the file to a company we knew that works specifically with import and export transactions: Smuggley, Swindol, &

Finkbottom Finance. Although we had never sent a prospect to Smuggley, they came highly recommended and were located not far from our office.

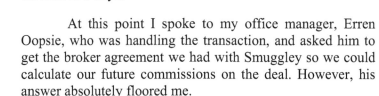

Upon receipt of the file, Smuggley went forward with their evaluation. After a few days, they informed us the client had a strong track record and their customers' credit ratings were outstanding. This was great news and we informed D.L. the file was progressing smoothly. Another few weeks passed and Smuggley informed us the prospect was in the process of signing closing documents and the deal would be funding in the next few days.

At this point I spoke to my office manager, Erren Oopsie, who was handling the transaction, and asked him to get the broker agreement we had with Smuggley so we could calculate our future commissions on the deal. However, his answer absolutely floored me.

Erren informed me he was working with Smuggley's lead salesperson, Gilbert Glibwerds, but never signed a formal agreement; they would just work that out after the deal closed. In essence, there was no formal contract in place between Smuggley, Swindol, & Finkbottom Finance and us. We were at their mercy to pay what Gilbert only verbally stated they would. But there was absolutely nothing in writing to protect us and ensure we would receive our commissions – which for a deal this size would be considerable.

I quickly called Gilbert, asked him to send us an agreement, and inquired what our broker commission was on the deal. He said that he was not sure and he would have to speak to his supervisor, Tank Hammerhed. This was a very bad omen.

When Gilbert hadn't responded after several days, I called Mr. Hammerhed, who said he was not aware of any broker arrangement with our company on this deal. Further, he said his company felt since they had done all the due diligence, the most we were entitled to receive was a very small referral fee. My worst fears were coming to pass.

In a very professional manner I told Tank of our discussions with Gilbert as a broker, and changing the story at this point was extremely unethical. His response was to rattle off several four letter words, and in no uncertain terms told me to take it or leave it.

We were up a creek without a paddle. Because no formal agreement was in place, Smuggley, Swindol, & Finkbottom Finance wasn't obligated to pay us a penny. Because I wanted to salvage some type of payment for D.L. Phinder, the original broker, I swallowed my pride and accepted their paltry referral fee.

The obvious lesson here is to always have a formal agreement in place with any funder *prior* to sending them a prospect for evaluation. If you don't, you can lose many, many thousands of dollars on a deal – just like we did on this one.

Comment

Another lesson is this: first be very careful to whom you send *any* deals, especially large ones! Even with written agreements in place, I've heard horror stories from brokers who said they had referred deals to factors or funders – and had a signed Broker Agreement – who a short time later unilaterally decided the broker just wasn't going to get paid. They knew if the broker (almost always a very small company) tried to sue, they had far more legal resources than the referrer, and could simply starve the person out. The broker wouldn't be able to afford a court battle, even if the unpaid commissions were sizeable.

This case study proves, quite painfully, not all factors and funders have high ethical standards. With any referral, be sure you are dealing with a company with integrity, and get it in writing. It's a jungle out there.

23.

Onin's Workouts & Isometric Exercise Systems (OWIES)

Rodrigo Ridadi
Front Range Factoring

Onin's Workouts & Isometric Exercise Systems (OWIES), was referred by another factor. The company provided personal training and wellness services to the Human Resources division at a large company, Obfuscation Fitness and Training (OFAT). Invoice terms were net 45.

Onin's Workouts & Isometric Exercises was brand new so there was no track record to be found on the business. The president of the company, Onin Barbells, had run several companies previously, but our background investigation found no obvious issues or concerns regarding those. Onin had a few judgments and a minor criminal offense from some 15 years prior.

$\boxed{\text{DD}}$

Initial due diligence showed no issues. Obfuscation Fitness and Training was a very large company with very good credit. Their relationship with OWIES was new with no billings outstanding, and their contract left little room for rebates or refunds.

$\boxed{\text{DD}}$

It appeared to be a clean deal, so I made a proposal which was accepted and we proceeded to sign the contract. When I notified OFAT, I learned the billing process was such that OWIES would receive an invoice approval number from OFAT even before billing which, according to OFAT's services buyer, was verification of services provided. I made sure I would be copied on these communications. OFAT's payables department acknowledged the Notice of Assignment; however it became apparent some of their payables were managed by a third party vendor, Giterdun Payment Services, and some were managed internally.

Although the OFAT's process seemed confusing, multiple parties inside the organization were receptive to the changes required by the factoring arrangement. Further, we received some indications that OWIE's invoices would likely be handled by Giterdun Payment Services, given their relatively small size.

I then opened an account with Giterdun, linked it to our client's existing account, and made sure all payments would be directed to Front Range Factoring. We still wanted to make sure OFAT's records showed Front Range as the payee for OWIES' invoices, and it seemed to be only a matter of time before this would be in place. So I became comfortable enough to fund the account only a few days after notifying the debtor.

Unfortunately, communications with OFAT's Accounts Payable staff were fractured throughout: they did not accept my calls or emails, only voice messages and emails into general inboxes. The actual person who was buying the services was helpful, but she did not have control over the payables process. We couldn't seem to get a straight answer as to whether the payments would be handled internally by OFAT or through Giterdun Payment Services,

nor whether the remittance address in OFAT's system had been updated. After many attempts over approximately three weeks, one response from OFAT's Accounts Payable showed that the remittance address had not been updated at all.

Further inquiries showed that, even later, still nothing had been done towards that goal. I continued insisting.

I escalated the issue with OFAT and learned their records could not be changed, as they were linked to the information in the contract. If payments originated with OFAT, they supposedly could only send checks to the address listed on the contract, and that a contract amendment would be required to change the remittance address. OFAT

was not receptive to amending the contract. However, I received additional indications that the payments would be handled by Giterdun Payment Services, and remittance information with them was already up to date.

By now, the first invoices were due, and we had not yet received payment. We contacted Onin, who confirmed he had received the check and had not deposited it. He sent the check and the invoices were settled; this confirmed that these payments were being handled internally by OFAT, not by Giterdun Payment Services. We contacted OFAT again, who agreed to submit payments through Giterdun from then on.

After seeking additional confirmation, Giterdun decided they wanted me to sign an agreement with them, basically to protect them in certain situations. During a somewhat onerous process we agreed to contract language that we both felt comfortable with. After this, we received periodic payments via EFT for factored invoices from Giterdun.

Lessons

1. Large account debtors can be good, and they can be bad.

2. In some cases, particularly in industries where factoring is prevalent, the good credit of a large debtor can offset the hassle of dealing with outsourced Accounts Payable call centers.

3. However, in industries where factoring is not prevalent, dealing with all the pieces in a heavily divided AP department can be very onerous.

4. Finally, having an honest client never hurts.

Comment

Rodrigo was lucky to have an honest client in this case. As we've seen (and will see), clients who receive factored checks just too easily deposit them, either in ignorance or in silence. Having a client who actually does the right thing – sending the checks to you – is the way it should be, but much too often isn't.

Working with very large companies can be quite a pain, as Rodrigo found. Signed contracts, amendments to contracts, and new contracts can all be part of simply getting paid for invoices you've purchased. A debtor like this makes you really appreciate the ones who understand factoring, pay you properly, and aren't a hassle to work with. When you deal with very large debtors who can be, as Rodrigo put it, "onerous" to deal with, you absolutely must have an honest client to start with. Otherwise, the formula:

Big Debtor + Disorganized AP Department + Checks Sent to Client + Dishonest Client = Loss of money.

Fortunately, in this equation Rodrigo had an honest client instead of a dishonest one, and all was well. However, that can change at any moment with any client, even one you've had for years – as we'll see in the next case study.

24.

Mr. Scumbucket Janitorial Company

Jeff Callender
Dash Point Financial

Mr. Scumbucket Janitorial Company, owned by Hyden Sneek, was located in the Southeast and referred by one of our best brokers, Fritz Findsem. Both Hyden and Fritz live in the same city, and Fritz had been to Hyden's office several times and felt he had great potential to become quite successful.

Hyden needed to factor about $10,000 per month to start. His customers were solid, the underwriting went smoothly, and he very much looked forward to factoring. We provided our standard rates and after the first few schedules, Hyden made a point of letting me know how much he appreciated what we were doing for his business. He sang our praises, saying how much factoring was not only helping his company but was even improving his health: his blood pressure had improved and he slept much better because he no longer worried about meeting payroll. His accolades made great reference material and he was more than happy to let us use his words on our website's Testimonials page.

155

While Hyden was extremely appreciative of our service, he did not want his customers to know he was factoring. Like many clients, he was concerned they would think he was in financial difficulty if they found out, and I agreed to work on a non-notification basis.[1] I even allowed him to pick up payment checks (a policy we *never* allow any more[2]) and overnight them to me the next day. Hyden dutifully faxed every check as soon as he obtained it, then overnighted it the same day. Seeing the checks on my doorstop without fail the following day made me feel warm and fuzzy about this account.

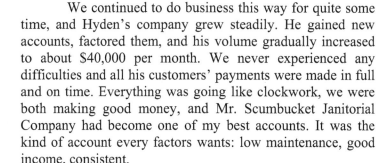

We continued to do business this way for quite some time, and Hyden's company grew steadily. He gained new accounts, factored them, and his volume gradually increased to about $40,000 per month. We never experienced any difficulties and all his customers' payments were made in full and on time. Everything was going like clockwork, we were both making good money, and Mr. Scumbucket Janitorial Company had become one of my best accounts. It was the kind of account every factors wants: low maintenance, good income, consistent.

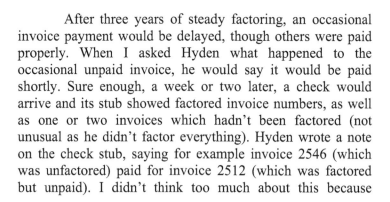

After three years of steady factoring, an occasional invoice payment would be delayed, though others were paid properly. When I asked Hyden what happened to the occasional unpaid invoice, he would say it would be paid shortly. Sure enough, a week or two later, a check would arrive and its stub showed factored invoice numbers, as well as one or two invoices which hadn't been factored (not unusual as he didn't factor everything). Hyden wrote a note on the check stub, saying for example invoice 2546 (which was unfactored) paid for invoice 2512 (which was factored but unpaid). I didn't think too much about this because

---

[1] I no longer do this; Dash Point is a full notification factor. After reading this book, I hope your practice is the same.

[2] Ditto.

everything he factored was being paid and we were making good money.

However, as time went by, these substitute payments occurred more frequently. Tracking which paid unfactored invoices were paying which unpaid factored invoices was becoming confusing. Finally we had about a dozen unpaid invoices that were being paid by unfactored ones, and I couldn't keep track of it anymore. Moreover, the substitute payments were lagging behind and we were now owed money. His escrow reserve account was being used to make up some of the shortfall, but at the rate these substitutions were going, it was a matter of time before that would be inadequate. I told Hyden this had to stop and we needed to get paid for the unpaid invoices with checks that had their invoice numbers on them – no more substitutions.

This made Hyden quite agitated and he said it had to continue. When I asked why, he said it was just the way he had to do business. Like the dimwit who's always last to get a joke, it dawned on me something fishy was going on and I suddenly had the sick feeling my star client was taking me for a ride. As a factor, this is one of those realizations that literally can make you feel like you're going to throw up.

Despite his insistence we not contact his customers, I had my coworker Veronica call them anyway. With the first phone call, she discovered over the past several months Hyden had picked up many checks (she obtained the check numbers from the customers) with one or two factored invoices on them that he had not overnighted to us. Not surprisingly, these invoices' payments were the ones being substituted with the unfactored payments.

Further, Veronica gave the AP people copies of invoices for which we had not been paid. After a little checking, they told her that they had no record of those invoices, but they did show that the jobs listed on the invoices had already been billed and paid from other invoices. In short, Hyden had been billing twice for several of the same jobs: one invoice was valid, the other bogus, and he factored both. Since we had developed a trust level with the account, we had not verified these invoices three years into the relationship. The sad truth of the matter was now clear: I had been played by Hyden Sneek, Mr. Scumbucket himself.

At this point we had about $30,000 in outstanding invoices. A day or two after Veronica's calls to his customers, Hyden called her, furious, and was actually menacing. He threatened her, saying he would sue her for "destroying his business" and damaging his relationship with his customers. Showing her pluck, Veronica responded she had every right to call the customers since we had purchased the invoices, we owned them, and he had assigned their payment to Dash Point. He shouted at her again she had no right to make those calls and slammed the phone down.

He called me immediately and made it quite clear he was enraged. I let him vent and said that we had several problem invoices that needed to be repaid. I told him Veronica would no longer deal with his account (I actually feared for her safety, despite the eleven hundred mile distance between them). Not only was Hyden one big dude, I didn't know what he might actually pull in this state of mind.

I told Hyden that because of what he had done (which he actually admitted once he calmed down a bit), we had to stop funding him immediately and work out a means to begin paying Dash Point back. He wasn't happy but it was clear his outburst at Veronica was because he had been caught red-handed defrauding us. Because he knew that I knew what had happened, he was more subdued.

We continued to collect from his customers who now paid us directly. Over the next month or so we received a few payments, leaving a balance of $25,000 he needed to repay. We applied the last $1,000 he had in escrow reserves to his debt, and I established a workout schedule in which he would pay us $250 per week until the remaining $24,000 was repaid. Hyden agreed to this and we made weekly ACH withdrawals from his bank account to which he also agreed. I much prefer this method over waiting for such a client to send a check. The first seven of these payments came through with no problem.

However, the next ACH was returned NSF, as were four of his next six payments – five out of seven total. The last NSF was the final blow to my patience, and I gave his account to my collection attorney, Cleaver Squeezem. Cleaver was happy to take on the account that now owed us a bit over $20,000, and he also worked out a payment arrangement with Hyden.

True to form, Hyden made the first few payments properly (by check to Cleaver) but they soon became farther apart, a few bounced, and eventually stopped. Cleaver (like any good lawyer) was eager to litigate. He felt we had an excellent chance of winning in court and collecting because 1) we had good documentation, 2) Hyden acknowledged he owed the money by virtue of the workout payments he had made, and 3) he had the assets of his still-in-business company. I could almost hear Cleaver salivating.

When Hyden learned that he was being sued for $20,000, he claimed that amount was more than it should have been (though he had no paperwork to back up his assertion). Surprisingly, he obtained a law firm, D'Lay, Obstrukt & Hindir (DOH), to fight our lawsuit. A couple months after we learned he had done this, D'Lay made the argument that because Dash Point Financial was located outside the state where Hyden lived, we had no jurisdiction there and the case should be dismissed. Cleaver and other factors I knew in Hyden's state said that argument was laughable and he clearly had no defense. He owed the money and his lawyer was just looking for a way to get him off the hook. It appeared he was grasping at straws but the fact that he was fighting us was not good. D'Lay knew how to play the system and this was not going to be easy.

Having never sued a client before, I didn't know exactly what to expect (though I knew none of it would be fun and all of it expensive) and quite honestly I wasn't very willing to go through with it. On the other hand, I certainly wanted my money back. Cleaver indicated the lawsuit had to be done in Hyden's city, and I would have to travel there to appear in court (not what I wanted to hear).

A few quick calculations made me hesitate – if we won, the amount my attorneys (both local representation and Cleaver) would keep would be 40%. That meant that in the best case scenario, *if* we won, and *if* we collected all $20,000 owed, I would end up with about $13,000 – exactly the amount of advances I was out of pocket. That was a lot of "if's" to just barely get my money back, and I wasn't convinced the whole effort was worth the trouble. Just writing off the $13,000 to bad debt seemed like the road of least resistance.

Hyden's city (and the location of the court proceedings) was two-thirds the way across the country from me. I was very reluctant since I didn't feel too well from some health issues I was having at the time. Nonetheless, Cleaver said that had to be done and obtained local counsel, Truman Tenacious of Tenacious & Durble, to represent my case. I prepared the boatload of paperwork and backup documents required, paid the required fees, and braced myself for an unpleasant experience. A court date was set.

Truman knew D'Lay and said he was a very sharp attorney; D'Lay and his associates at DOH would do everything to help Hyden win. True enough, he filed two continuances, postponing the trial 60 days each time, in hopes I would drop the suit. Finally the third (and last) court date was set and I had to show up. The more this dragged on the less enthusiasm (if I had any to start) I felt. I had no doubt D'Lay was counting on that.

Unfortunately, shortly before the final court date I injured my knee and had to have surgery. That meant not only travelling while still not feeling well, but going across country with a very sore post-surgical knee and a cane. I finally told Truman I couldn't make it to court and asked if Fritz Findsem could be there as my representative. Truman wasn't too thrilled with the idea since Fritz hadn't been in on the transactions except to receive his commissions. But Truman decided to continue the case in hopes that Hyden or D'Lay would make a blunder. Truman went ahead with the court date and appeared without me. Much to our surprise, Hyden didn't show up in court; and because of his absence, we won a default judgment for the $20,000. We were jubilant!

However, this was far from over. D'Lay, Obstrukt & Hindir's next move? *File an appeal!* Good grief. Hyden's attorney fees by now had to be close to what he owed me, and simple logic suggested he would be smart to seek a settlement and end the ordeal; but I assumed D'Lay convinced Hyden not to do that since he thought he could just wait me out. (Besides, DOH wouldn't make as much in fees if Hyden settled. Better for them to drag out the case as long as possible.) I was learning first-hand why major court cases take many years and cost sky-high amounts in legal fees. My relatively small suit has slogged through the system for a couple years now, and we still hadn't seen a dime, though at least we won. Sort of.

Fast forward through the appeals process (another several months). One day, out of the blue, Cleaver called me with a cheerful voice and told me the judge tossed out D'Lay's motion for appeal, which meant we had at last, once and for all, won. There were no other legal maneuvers available and the case was final. Now all we had to do was collect.

I was required to pay Tenacious & Durble another $300 to begin the final collections proceedings, which involved garnishing any assets Truman can get his hands on – bank accounts, property, vans, etc. Repossessing assets, like vans, means the Sheriff would impound the vehicle/s and sell it/them at auction. Unfortunately, as Truman began his search for assets, he told us he wasn't finding any in Hyden Sneek's or the company's names. However, he did find another side of this man we hadn't known.

He suggested we look at his Facebook page. Why, oh why, hadn't we thought to look there sooner?! Hyden's his identifying picture on his Facebook page was a large photo of Las Vegas, obviously taken by Mr. Sneek himself. There were many more pictures of him there, clearly having a great time. But that was just for starters.

The page also had photo albums with multiple pictures of him on cruises, and other albums showing him enjoying many hours on the golf course. Included were two brief videos of him on the links with a friend, showing off his golf swing which he obviously had been working on. (They also showed he wasn't a natural athlete, to put it nicely.)

His Likes included five folders, each named by year and each with the Likes he'd entered each year; he had been making these entries for quite some time. Each of these yearly folders included cruises and his membership in the country club. They also mentioned the Daily Jesus site, from which he apparently obtained regular inspiration and strength.

What's more, this page had a link to his business website, which when clicked, opened with a link to a short video advertisement for the Better Business Bureau. Curious, I clicked to see if his company might be mentioned. Sure enough, the video showed a list of, and the narrative voice extolled, a few of the wonderful businesses in his city, and of course Mr. Scumbucket Janitorial was the last of the fine companies mentioned.

The rest of his site was obviously very expensive and professionally done. Among other things, it showed a picture of one of his workers in a uniform with the company logo on his back. As you perused the pages, you certainly felt like this was a company of high repute and trustworthiness.

As I poured over his website and Facebook pages, which dated back to the time he had been defrauding me and fighting the lawsuit, I felt my blood boiling. I couldn't believe he had the nerve to post, for years, these pictures and brag with impudent, arrogant swagger about his lifestyle. His enjoyment of the high life (almost certainly fueled by his fraud) – and the fact that he had been living this way for at least five years – all illustrated what an absolute scumbucket this man was.

Since he clearly has learned to play the game, I have no doubt his assets are securely hidden in someone else's name or offshore, and getting any money from him is going to be very difficult if not impossible. IRS has a new $14,000 lien in place, as well.

Clearly, utilizing the Justice system doesn't always end with justice for the victim. And this is what you endure when you deal with a business like Mr. Scumbucket Janitorial Company and a person like Hyden Sneek.

Comment

As we have seen in other case studies, when the factor knows something isn't right with an account, and the client gets riled when the factor talks directly to customers (or even suggests doing so), this is a sure indication the client has committed fraud. He doesn't want you talking to the customer because he knows if you do, he'll be found out. We saw this here with Hyden Sneek, as well as other case studies:

- Dee Seetful in Case Study 3, Dee Seetful and Associates
- Lem Ecollum in Case Study 11, BudiBuddy Metal Fabrication
- Wrangle Clank in Case Study 19, Clank Brothers Wiring and Cable.

Additionally, this case study shows that even though a bad practice (letting a client obtain checks) may work for a very long time, it's far better to utilize the correct procedure from the beginning. If I had done this, chances are much less that Hyden would've defrauded me – at least so easily.

It's also a lesson in doing ongoing due diligence on a client especially when things go bad. Sites like Facebook provide windows into the personal lives of prospects and clients, and you absolutely must utilize these sites. I never cease to be amazed at what people will put on their Facebook pages, and Hyden Sneek took this to a whole new level. His brazenness was just unbelievable, given what he was doing the whole time he posted his pictures and updates. If I had just once thought to look him up there, I would have understood what kind of person he was, and avoided a huge amount of stress and loss of time and money.

This case study also illustrates how our legal system often works. A person does something questionable or wrong (Hyden in this case – in other examples, Case Study 7, SmallFrey Alarm Company, and Case Study 16, Audacity Cleaning Service). The person hires a lawyer to defend him, and the attorney comes up with a justification or a legal maneuver (or numerous legal maneuvers) to absolve his client of responsibility. This has nothing to do with making sure that true justice prevails, but with protecting the person or company paying the attorney to get the wrongdoer off the hook.

This is a client I will never forget, both because he was such a good client for so long, as well as the anguish he put me through trying to collect a debt he acknowledged he owed by agreeing to two different workouts. His true nature revealed on his Facebook page posted throughout my ordeal make him one of the most detestable human beings I've ever known.

Just like we saw in Case Study 20, HAWLIT, you just never know which clients are going to be bad or good. You also don't know which good clients are going to stay that way.

25.

Safensound Janitorial and Maintenance

Melissa Donald
LDI Growth Partners

Safensound Janitorial and Maintenance was referred to us by a salesperson/broker with whom my partner and I formerly worked. The company provides janitorial and maintenance service exclusively to the food warehouse industry. Their customers are huge, multinational food distributors and supermarket chains. Safensound had a long standing relationship with another fairly local factoring firm, but was experiencing some challenges with their operations procedures and wanted to talk to someone else to see what was out there.

I met the principal, Merv S. Tic, and his then-fiancée (now wife) Fran, at a local coffee shop and just got to know them. I explained why their current factor was doing some of the things they were doing and we discussed whether it would be cost effective or reasonable to make a change. Their current contract had a pricey termination penalty, and even though our standard pricing (which is daily rather than incremental) would save them some money over time, it would take more than a year to "earn back" the termination penalty they would have to pay to leave. It was my recommendation that they try to renegotiate their contract with their existing factor as it seemed prohibitive to make a change.

A year later, while I was working to launch a new chapter of BNI (Business Network International, www.BNI.com), I ran into Fran, who was joining the new group for her business. Over the next year, we spent quite a bit of time together as she became one of the leaders of the group and I was working with her on a regular basis.

A year after Fran joined BNI, I received an urgent phone call that something had gone terribly wrong with their existing factoring relationship. They were not receiving phone calls back, regularly scheduled advances were not being funded and well-seasoned reserves were not being released. In the janitorial business, the invoices are almost exclusively payroll related, with a slim to moderate margin.

In the time since we first met and that frantic phone call, LDI had gone through a change in the kinds of deals we were looking for. We were focusing our efforts on companies doing under $1M in sales. Safensound was well on its way to $3M in sales. To say it would be a stretch for us to accommodate a deal that size was an understatement, plus we would not have the usual ramp-up period into a new deal as we would be taking out the existing factor. The situation could have been really scary for us.

Why wasn't it scary? And why were we even considering breaking our own model to do it? I knew them. I sat across from Fran for lunch at least once a month. We talked. We emailed. I had been following their progress and challenges for a couple years. I could not have been more comfortable.

We moved fast. Less than a week passed from the frantic phone call, to wires going out for both the payoff to the other factor, and initial funding to the client. We cut corners that for us are usually not negotiable (such as sending notifications and initial funding verifications after advancing, rather than before). Did we hold our breath? Of course. We always do for a new client. In this case, however, we just knew it was going to be okay.

They quickly became one of our anchor clients. Their accounts pay via ACH and rarely does a payment arrive after 30 days.

We are now approaching the two year mark in our factoring relationship with Merv and Fran. I have been working with them for the last six months to make sure they have all their ducks in a row to transition away from factoring and into bank financing. I expect that we will barely celebrate our second anniversary before they move on. It has been a

lucrative and positive experience for all of us and our association will continue long after they leave the LDI fold.

Comment

This is another example of taking a chance and having it pay off. In this case, Melissa didn't see the risk as large (despite the size of the factoring volume) because of her relationship with Fran through BNI, and being in close, regular in-person contact. However, just the size of the deal would have been enough to preclude many small factors from accepting the deal.

Could things have gone south with this deal? Things can go south with *any* deal, as we just saw with Mr. Scumbucket. Yet Melissa had an ace up her sleeve with this client that doesn't usually exist with others: a close working relationship through BNI. Had Fran pulled a fast one on Melissa, Fran's standing in BNI would have been destroyed and many referrals lost (at best). Further, these were extremely solid debtors who paid dependably, like clockwork.

While there was plenty for Melissa to lose with this client, her confidence was well founded.

26.

Slimegall Medical Transport

Jeff Callender
Dash Point Financial

Slimegall Medical Transport was a company owned by Bligh Slimegall, a man in his mid-50's who found my website searching for a factor. He had been in business for about a year and provided medical transportation services to doctor and hospital appointments for older patients who could not get to the appointments on their own.

Bligh's service was paid for by a state agency, Payurides, so underwriting the debtor didn't involve much. Bligh's personal and business underwriting showed only a few small state tax liens, most of which had been released. We set up his account, received the signed NOA from a payables staff person at Payurides, and were ready to go.

His receivables totaled about $12,000 monthly. He wanted to factor to have steady cash flow since he was paid monthly by Payurides, and needed to pay for gas and operating expenses every day. The only catch was this: he earned between $10 to $25 per trip, and every day he had multiple trips and numerous people he was transporting. In a given day, he would have forty or fifty trips, for each of which he logged the person's name and amount. So by the end of a week, his log would be many pages long (single spaced), with line after line after line of $10 and $25 charges. Each week these would add up to about $2,000 to $4,000.

Obviously we couldn't track every charge for every trip, so we batched his weekly totals and called a weekly batch an invoice. Beginning the first week of February, each Friday he submitted his trip logs so we saw every trip for which he was charging, and advanced him on that week's total. He would also submit this paperwork to Payurides who paid via ACH deposit into Dash Point's bank account at the beginning of each month. While these payments arrived like clockwork, we never received notification from Payurides as to which trips (or weeks) the payments covered; we simply saw the amount deposited in our bank account. Every monthly payment was always a different amount and never a round number, and all were consistent and roughly the amount being factored the previous month. Because we couldn't track the payments to specific trips, we applied the payments to the oldest invoices in the system. This seemed to work and we followed this procedure for the rest of the year.

However, by spring – about three or four months after he started factoring – we noticed the number of days Payurides was taking to pay was increasing. While the first several batches were paid in 30 days the first couple months, they were now starting to take forty or fifty days, even though we continued receiving an ACH at the beginning of each month. As time went on, this pattern continued and by summer the oldest invoices were past 60 days. We asked Bligh why this was so and he just shrugged it off and said, "Well, it's a state agency. You know how slow those can be." Because the monthly amounts continued to come in very consistently, we continued funding.

By fall the lateness of the oldest batches was becoming alarming. They were now past 90 days and we were using his escrow reserves to cover recoursed batches. Other than the signed NOA we'd received almost a year earlier, we had no contact person at Payurides. Bligh kept saying they were a state agency who was behind in their paperwork, and kept factoring every Friday. We continued to fund through the end of the year and at that point were owed in the neighborhood of $50,000 for his account.

In January we didn't receive the expected ACH deposit from Payurides and Bligh uncharacteristically didn't return our calls. I called Payurides, and spoke with the person who signed the NOA, Fletcher Flunkey. When asked why we hadn't received payment as usual, Fletcher quickly referred me to the AP supervisor, Sheeda Boss. I asked Sheeda why we hadn't received the ACH deposit at the beginning of the month as usual. Sheeda said she needed to look into it and would get back to me. A few days later she did, and had some unbelievable news.

"At the beginning of the year, Mr. Slimegall directed us to pay the January ACH to him, which we did." I was flabbergasted. I told her we had the NOA signed by Fletcher which clearly instructed Payuride to pay only Dash Point, and only an officer of Dash Point could release the NOA. I sent her a copy of the signed NOA, and after reading it she replied, "Yes, it looks like we shouldn't have done that." I resisted the urge to scream *"Well DUH, lady!"* and was glad to actually have someone in authority admit her department had messed up. However, I was more concerned about the whole $50,000 we were owed.

I told her how much we were owed and asked the amount of the diverted January ACH payment. She said it was about $5,000. "But what about the other $45,000?" I asked. "Well, $5,000 is all we owed," she said. This was taking a very sickening turn. "How could you only owe five thousand? I'm owed fifty thousand, not five!" I implored.

She informed me all the amounts Payurides approved for payment, and in fact paid, were documented on their website and every provider had access to it. She seemed a bit surprised I didn't know about this site. "All you have to do is log in and see every trip we've approved for payment, and every trip not approved." Indeed, all year long they had paid every approved trip, so she was right – they didn't owe any of the remaining $45,000. Over the course of the year, that many trips had not been approved; I just didn't know it until that moment. She concluded, "Everything owed for his account has been paid and there is nothing more due."

Bligh Slimegall had pulled an incredible heist.

During the eleven months we had been funding him, he never informed me this website existed, never told me any rides were not approved, and never even hinted Payurides wasn't going to pay everything he was factoring. He blithely submitted his trip logs every week and took his advances *knowing* about 25% of his trips had not been approved, and that many more were *not going to be* paid. Redirecting the January payment was the final coup of his year-long fraud. He knew exactly what he was doing and kept the gravy train going week after week, month after month, without the slightest indication to me or Veronica of what he was pulling. He was a brazen, unscrupulous thief with incredible gall – as most genuine crooks are.

During our conversation, Sheeda Boss understood the fraud Bligh had pulled and she was clearly done with him. I asked if any more payments were going to be made for his account, and she said, "No. Now that we know what he's done he won't be driving for us anymore." Slimegall Medical Transport's contract was summarily terminated by Payurides.

While Payurides was finished with Slimegall, I wasn't finished with Payurides. Because they had not only paid over notice but Sheeda Boss actually admitted doing so, I told her they were now obligated to pay Dash Point according to UCC law. At first she acknowledged that would happen, but over the next few weeks no $5,000 payment appeared. I called her to ask when this would be sent, and she said she had to run this by counsel before that could happen. "Oh, great," I thought. "Just what I wanted to hear." I knew all too well that the job of a debtor's attorney's is to figure out how to get his client off the hook when they've done the wrong thing.

Now that an attorney was involved, I gave the account to my collection attorney, Cleaver Squeezem. I had come to learn that a lawyer-to-lawyer conversations usually got things done much quicker than my trying to convince a lawyer I knew more about UCC law than he did, especially if he wouldn't admit he was clueless about it. After a couple months of attorney discussions, Cleaver squeezed a $5,000 check from Payurides and I at least had that much satisfaction. However, I was still out $45,000. That would have to come from Bligh Slimegall. Wonderful.

Cleaver tried several times to contact Bligh who of course had vanished into the mist. Despite the amount, and probably because he felt Bligh had no money anyway, Cleaver gave up and said it was uncollectible. I gave the account to our collection agency Onus, Dred, & Trembal. They made a (rather feeble) attempt to contact Bligh and gave up too.

This whole experience is a major frustration, to say the least, but shows how such an incredibly dishonest person can disappear and just waltz away from criminal behavior. Bligh Slimegall is one slimeball I'd really like to nail. He deserves to be parked in a jail cell for a long time, but I realize that will never happen.

I'm sure he does, too.

Comment

This case study is another lesson in taking action when you notice something has changed slightly: payments are not as regular, or in the amounts you expect, or start taking longer and longer to pay than they once did. When any of these happen, call the debtor immediately and find out why. Because I was being paid regularly this red flag failed to get my attention, and (to my regret) I continued to fund this crook week after week after week.

Had I contacted Payurides months earlier, I would have immediately learned about their website and found the fraud Bligh was perpetuating. He would not have diverted funds, and the arrearage with Payurides (and my loss) would have been considerably smaller.

This is also a lesson in asking about payment websites, especially with government and very large customers. More and more organizations have these sites. As we've seen with other case studies (#6 Claire's Repairs, #8 Razzle & Dazzle Manufacturing, #14 Sloppee Properties, and #15 Gogetter Property Services), using them is a tremendous risk mitigator for any factor. Thus, a step on your underwriting checklist for new prospects must be to learn if such a website exists for any customer.

Always ask very early (of both the prospect and the customer) if the debtor has a web site to track payments and/or other AP functions. If I had asked that simple question before I advanced a penny, chances are this account could have actually been a good one and I would have made out nicely instead of having a nasty write off.

This case study also provides a perfect illustration of a mistake that's very easy to make as a factor. In the book *How to Run a Small Factoring Business*, there is a chapter called "Common Mistakes," and one of the 24 common mistakes mentioned is this one: "Blindly Batching Invoices."

Batching invoices when you can track every invoice that has been batched, or at least know when part of a batch of invoices is not going to be paid, can work. But when you have no idea which invoices and/or batches you're being paid for – and which ones aren't being paid at all (as was the case here) – the result is that invoices appear to be paying more and more slowly. It's only a matter of time before you realize you're in the deep, dark hole and can't get out of it.

Especially when the person who put you there is a creep like Bligh Slimegall.

27.
Methodical
Manufacturing

Jeff Callender
Dash Point Financial

Methodical Manufacturing is a children's furniture manufacturing company referred a few years ago by a larger local factor who found the volume too low to meet their parameters. Owner Darrell Adept is a soft-spoken and smart businessman who oversees the operation. He is assisted by his daughter Adelle who manages the billing and bookkeeping, and another man who handles sales. His products are made in his plant which is about 45 minutes from my home.

Methodical's high-quality children's furniture is sold to preschools, community centers, Native American tribes around the state, and online and catalogue children's furniture and sports equipment resellers. His customers usually pay in about 30 - 40 days, though some go out to around 60. Getting NOAs in place is not an issue as Adelle is very helpful preparing their customers for our letter. While payment over notice happens occasionally (though never due to her instructions to customers), she always follows protocol. When a check is sent to her, she faxes a copy so we know it's coming, then mails it immediately to our lock box where it usually arrives in a day because it doesn't have far to go. She has never deposited a check paying a factored invoice and I can't imagine she ever would. If that did happen, I could quickly pay them a visit since they are local.

Darrell wanted to factor because the volume of his orders was increasing and he needed to keep his production steady by maintaining inventory levels. Keeping his inventory regularly replenished enables him to fill orders of any size without delays or cash flow issues. During our initial conversation I felt as if he were interviewing me as much as I was interviewing him. He made the comment he likes to work with local businesses as much as possible, thus his interest in using Dash Point Financial. My normal discount rate was slightly higher than other (nonlocal) factors he considered, but we were able to negotiate an amount that satisfied us both. While I normally don't negotiate my rates, in this one case I made an exception because his volume was somewhat higher than usual for me, he was local, and he impressed me as a sharp businessman who ran his company wisely, calmly, and without drama.

His invoices are typically several hundred dollars to about $25,000 in size, though most are in the $2,000 to $10,000 range. His volume fluctuates somewhat; at times he may have nothing or perhaps $10,000 outstanding, but can go up to about $50,000 in open receivables. He has a good amount of business he doesn't need to factor. When he is considering a new prospective customer, he has me check their credit before getting too far into negotiations, which helps him decide whether to accept them in the first place, and whether to factor their invoices if he does.

His customers typically pay in about 30 to 45 days, though some have gone out to 60 or more. Adelle is very helpful dealing with slower paying invoices, and her pleasant manner and excellent working relationship with her customers usually results in a prompt payment after her contact. We have never had to charge back an invoice because they don't reach 90 days. If recourse were required, they would be able to replace it with a new invoice and/or from the consistently healthy escrow reserve we keep.

I have often said to my coworkers, "I'll take a couple dozen more clients just like Darrell and Adelle." They run a sound, well-managed business, are a pleasure to work with, and have good customers who pay in full and on time. I can visit them in person any time I want, and I've never worried about getting paid back with their account. If only my whole portfolio were like this!

Comment

Here again we see what makes a desirable client.

- The owner is smart, wise, calm and without drama.
- Dependable staff. In this case they immediately fax, then mail, factored checks they occasionally receive.
- Customers pay well.
- The business is on solid footing and Darrell factors to add even more stability.
- Their factoring volume is not so large as to be risky, but large enough so the factor makes decent income.
- The client is local so an in-person visit is easy whenever needed.

If only we knew *before* we funded new clients whether or not they would have such good characteristics!

28.

Damon Deevyus, LLC

Jeff Callender
Dash Point Financial

Damon Deevyus, LLC, a small janitorial company in the Midwest, was owned by a 23-year-old man after whom the company was named. This client was referred by a broker, Vail N. Obscurity with whom I never had direct contact; instead, she simply referred Damon's father Dudley to me, and all discussions at the beginning included only Dudley and myself. During the life of the account I paid Vail commissions as they were earned, but I thought it odd she never once contacted me. I soon had my hands quite full with the account and had no reason to contact her. If Vail provides another referral in the future (which I don't expect), I'll refuse it in a heartbeat.

Dudley was in his 50's and quickly impressed me as an experienced and astute businessman. He had run successful companies and now was helping his son Damon grow his own firm by handling the marketing and arranging financing for him. Dudley lined up accounts and gave advice to Damon as to how to run the operation. Damon did the labor and billing, and I didn't speak to him until after factoring had actually started. When I did speak to him, I found him personable, friendly, and energetic.

During my first conversation with Dudley, he explained his son's business and described some of the companies he had run himself. Now his focus was on helping Damon succeed. The company needed to factor because of the typical 30 – 45 wait for payments from his stable and established customers. However, Damon's company had a significant problem on its hands, and the tension and urgency in Dudley's voice told me he needed to resolve it quickly. The problem was the current factor he was using.

This factor, Duefuss, Inept & Pathetic, Inc. (DIPI), had been in business for a very long time and their name is well known in factoring circles. I had never dealt with them personally, however, and I quickly learned more about the company than I really wanted to know.

Dudley explained that DIPI was absolutely impossible to work with. He described his numerous frustrations starting with multiple phone calls to the account executive that were never returned. He attempted to contact the primary owner, Rufus Duefuss, to tell him of the problems with the AE's lack of response; but he never returned any calls either. The company would send Damon's advances and rebates only by overnighted checks (separately), for which he was charged $24 per check. Wires or ACH deposits were not offered, and every time they needed money, regardless of how small the amount, a check was overnighted. For a company as small as Damon's was, that became quite expensive (though earned wonderful extra fees for DIPI).

Dudley complained the discount rates' calculation was completely confusing, advances always unpredictable, and rebates usually remained unpaid. Factoring reports (even when he requested them several times) were rarely provided. Thus he never really knew the status of his account, which invoices had paid, and basically anything he needed to know to manage the business. Oh, and DIPI regularly slapped on hidden fees that seemed to come out of nowhere. In short, the relationship was miserable and he needed to terminate it as quickly as possible.

However, Damon's company still needed to factor; so this experienced businessman was looking for a different provider who would be dependable, available, provide timely reports, and have understandable discounts and reasonable charges. He was so anxious to get a new factor he wasn't too concerned about the rates; he just wanted a factor who would actually help him — not make running the business next to impossible. Anything would be better than what he had, he told me.

I am usually quite wary of taking on a client who is already factoring because too often the result is beneficial only for the client. What typically happens is this: the current factor (if the client is a good one) wants to keep the account so when the client says he's going to another factor, the current factor lowers his discount. Because his rate is now lower, the client decides to stay put. Now the factor is irritated with me for trying to poach his client, plus the fact that I have caused him to earn less income from the account. I get nothing but a waste of my time and a colleague who now doesn't like me. Therefore, I usually dismiss calls from currently factoring clients who are looking for a better rate. Nothing good is going to come of that, at least for me and the other factor.

However, Dudley's case was different, even compelling. I sensed everything he was saying was true and he wasn't just fishing for cheaper rates. In his case, the current factor really *was* a disaster and absolutely impossible to deal with. I was soon to find out first-hand just how true that assessment was.

I asked Dudley for a copy of the contract to see the rates he was being charged, and especially to learn if he was locked into a term contract which would be difficult to exit. When he sent the document, red flags (on the factor) immediately whipped high and hard. The contract, about three pages in length, was printed in an extremely tiny font that was so small I had to enlarge it to 200% just to read it. The margins were very narrow, the text tightly crammed together, and reading it even enlarged was visually not easy. Factors who make their contracts this difficult to read (to say nothing of the legal gibberish the document usually contains, as this one did) always make me nervous even before taking in a single word of the text.

As I read each section, more alarms went off. The rates were extremely convoluted, written in very confusing language, and even after reading them several times, I – an experienced factor myself – was equally befuddled as to just what he was paying. Indeed, there was no mention (as Dudley said) of required overnighted checks, and the hidden fees were so numerous – and ridiculous – I almost couldn't believe what I was reading. In short, this was a factoring contract from hell.

I was amazed Duefuss, Inept & Pathetic, Inc. had any clients at all, and found quite remarkable the fact they had been in business as long as they had. "How do they manage to book – and retain – *any* clients?" I wondered. It was a lesson that people badly in need of money will often settle on the first factor they find. DIPI's rates, while confusing, were not especially competitive, and it was clear they were resting on the laurels of being in business for a very long time.

Indeed, their marketing and promotions emphasized their longevity, and I saw from the contract and talking with Dudley they had absolutely nothing else to offer. DIPI apparently had plenty of money, but absolutely horrendous service. Dudley's story not only held up, I agreed he needed to get out of this catastrophe as quickly as possible.

Fortunately (and remarkably, considering everything else), there was no term to the contract and no penalty for leaving. I gave Dudley that shred of good news and began making preparations for a buyout. Determining exactly which invoices were still outstanding was not easy because he had been given no current reports, and my calls to Duefuss, Inept & Pathetic to discuss the buyout were – just like Dudley's – not returned. However he estimated there was no more than about $8,000 in factored invoices outstanding (he had been factoring as little as possible in anticipation of the change), so the buyout thankfully didn't involve a large sum.

After many attempts we finally secured a report showing the unpaid invoices, and the amount DIPI was owed as of the buyout date (which, to my astonishment, they had trouble calculating). Their NOAs were released (by me at their request), and my NOAs put in place. All the needed paperwork was signed (at which point I finally spoke with Damon), and the buyout funds sent to DIPI. We were at last under way.

Damon had good accounts and we factored about $20,000 - $30,000 per month for several months. Things went well, but a short time after we started Damon told me his father Dudley was having health problems and had left the company. I felt a slight twinge of unease at the thought Dudley was out of the picture and the company was now completely in the hands of this quite inexperienced young man. I liked Dudley and trusted his skills and perspective; he was a big reason I took on the account in the first place. Damon was an unknown entity and seemed quite wet behind the ears as far as running a business.

After a while, some of Damon's customers started short-paying a few of his invoices. We weren't too concerned about this as he had escrow reserve funds to cover the shortfalls. But over time these short payments increased in number and size, and some invoices were not being paid at all. We asked Damon why this might be happening, and he said he didn't know. So we started to call the account debtors to find out.

We soon learned that some of the invoices included in the buyout had been paid to Duefuss, Inept & Pathetic despite the NOA release and redirection to Dash Point. I called DIPI and after many attempts was finally able to speak with the finance person responsible for sending money. For some reason they had great trouble tracking down these payments, despite the fact I gave her the debtor names, check numbers, and check dates. After a few weeks she acknowledged we were owed the funds and sent a check. However, two invoices for about $1,000 apiece from the buyout remained unpaid and I would have to get those from DIPI later...I hoped.

Meanwhile, we learned from debtors who had short paid or not paid various invoices that this had occured because of three reasons: either 1) the work had not been completed, 2) the work was done poorly, or 3) they had been previously billed (and had paid) for the same work on earlier invoices. When we asked Damon about this, he was evasive and insisted the debtors were wrong and the invoices were fine. Our intuition was to trust the debtors as Damon's position, though consistent, was beginning to resemble Swiss cheese[1].

The more we spoke with the customers, the more our trust in Damon eroded. A couple AP people who had worked with him told us frankly he had been dishonest with them before we entered the picture. Double billings and shoddy work were not unusual, and a couple people (who had no decision making power as to which vendors they used) mentioned if they had any say they'd terminate his contract.

This news was unsettling to say the least, and we quickly contacted all debtors, even those who were paying properly. He soon lost some of these accounts, we assumed for the same reasons. The chargebacks we continued to take were putting a big dent in his advances and rebates, and Damon complained we weren't giving him enough money to run his business. We responded the reason for the chargebacks was his frequent billing errors and the fact that we weren't being paid enough by his customers to cover what we were owed. His escrow reserve was depleted and the only place we could get any funds were his advances. If he had actually done the work as the invoices stated the problem wouldn't have developed. Unfortunately, at that point the

---

[1] Full of holes.

horses were already out of the barn and we knew we had a problem.

Damon was becoming openly hostile to us and I tried to contact Dudley one last time in the outside chance he would intervene and talk some sense into his son. Unfortunately Dudley had become a complete...well, dud... and never once replied. Realizing Damon was starting to get desperate and knowing (based on the AP people's comments) his propensity to be sneaky and devious, we made sure every debtor once again acknowledged our NOA. We received assurances they would pay only us (directly) and not Damon, even if he tried to redirect payments – which we fully expected he would. It was then we learned he had picked up and deposited a couple checks already without telling us, at which point we terminated the contract, declared his account in default, and notified him he was responsible for all funds we were owed.

We continued to press the debtors to pay us for the remaining invoices, and they trickled in. We found the two remaining unpaid $1,000 invoices from the buyout had actually been paid long ago, a couple weeks after the buyout, to...well, who else but Duefuss, Inept & Pathetic? The debtor provided copies of the two checks, both clearly endorsed by DIPI about seven months earlier.

The few remaining contracts Damon had were terminated by his customers, and we were still owed about $12,000. In full collection mode, we started pressing DIPI for the $2,000 they'd received (and had no inkling of). We also made almost daily calls to the remaining debtor, Flakey Systems Corporation. The last few unpaid invoices they acknowledged were due made up the other $10,000. We spoke with the head of the AP department at Flakey Systems' headquarters which was located in a different state from Damon, and she repeatedly assured us they would send the check to our lock box. The check was due to be cut in a few days and she would personally make sure it came to us.

A week passed and the check still hadn't arrived. Meanwhile I continued to contact Duefuss, Inept & Pathetic numerous times to get the $2,000 from them, but to no avail (what a shock). I was getting nervous we would never see any of the funds we were owed. Finally we called the debtor and said we had not received the check. She said she would look into it and call us back. She did, and we couldn't believe our ears.

Damon Deevyus had lived up to his name. Just before headquarters cut our check, he went to the company's local branch in his town (where he had done the work) and told them he was owed payment for the last couple invoices totaling about $10,000. The clerk there looked up the records, and sure enough, saw the money was due. Without contacting headquarters, she cut the check and handed it to Damon. He cashed it immediately, before headquarters knew what the branch clerk had done and could put a stop payment on it. He'd pulled off a clever $10,000 heist right under their nose, and was gone.

Needless to say, we never heard from Damon again. He completely disappeared and our collection attorney, Cleaver Squeezem, couldn't find him. Sometimes I can almost hear his mocking, fiendish laughter cackling in the shadows.

Flakey Systems resisted our efforts to make them pay us since they had paid over notice, and even Cleaver Squeezem's efforts to get them to pay were fruitless. (They declared bankruptcy some time later.) It wasn't a large enough amount to litigate given attorney and court costs, and the only thing left was to try to get the remaining $2,000 from our wonderful colleagues at Duefuss, Inept & Pathetic, Inc.

I spent the next several months trying to do just that. Every time I called and asked to speak to the finance person, I was put on hold for 15 to 20 minutes, during which time I was forced to listen to their unbelievably obnoxious, unctuous, and self-serving phone message extolling how long they had been in business and how great they were. I called so many times, and was put on hold so long, that the 20-minute (I timed it after about the tenth call) message actually started repeating on a couple calls. After a while I had the first few minutes of the message memorized. I felt like I was undergoing some kind of mind control torture, listening to this message over and over and over.

Finally I tried to speak with the owner, Rufus, and was again placed on hold several times. One time I was told he was in a meeting and would be out in about ten minutes, and was asked if I would like to hold. I candidly said "no" but would anyway because he was so hard to reach, and at least the receptionist knew I was waiting. After listening to the mind-numbing message for the next half hour, I hung up and called right back. I was told Rufus had left for the day some time ago.

After a couple months of fruitless phone calls, Rufus Duefuss actually called me back. He was clearly unaware they had received any checks for this account (despite my telling him several times the checks had been sent seven months earlier, shortly after the buyout). He said that tracking a check which supposedly arrived that long ago would be very difficult, despite the fact I had sent him copies of both checks – which were endorsed by DIPI. He said not to contact his financial person anymore (I gathered she complained I was calling so much) because he would take care of this matter himself.

After waiting another three months and receiving nothing – no check, no phone calls, no email, no follow up – I was at the end of my rope with Duefuss. While the amount wasn't very much, only $2,000, it was the principal of this ludicrous escapade that had gotten to me. I decided to do something I had never done before (because I never *needed* to do it before) – I gave the $2,000 debt to Cleaver Squeezem.

He remembered the account since he had tried to collect from the debtor, Flakey Systems Corporation, and was dumbfounded I had had such an experience with a fellow factor. I gave him the check copies, buyout agreement, and anything else he asked for, and prepared him for the frustrations of trying to reach anyone in the Duefuss office, especially Rufus himself. I even quoted verbatim, with perfect voice intonations and inflections, the first twenty seconds of their on-hold phone message. He chuckled, saw this as something of a challenge, and plowed ahead.

A few weeks later Cleaver called me. His first words were, "Man, he really *is* hard to reach." I quietly agreed. He went on, "Duefuss thought this had been paid a long time ago and was very surprised to hear he owed anything." I shook my head, incredulous yet unsurprised. "But I think he was kind of embarrassed that I [a collection attorney sent from another factor] had called him about this, and he said he would take care of it." That last phrase made me a bit nervous because they were the exact words Rufus had said to me when I last talked to him four months previously.

However, almost beyond belief, about a month later a check arrived at Cleaver's office. Not surprisingly, the amount wasn't quite right – I had sent him *copies of the checks*, for Pete's sake – but it was close enough. Cleaver kept his cut and mailed me a check for the balance and I finally was able to close the last chapter on this very sorry and prolonged saga.

What have I learned from this experience? Needless to say, I will **never** deal with Duefuss, Inept, & Pathetic again. Even if a pleading client comes to me and begs me to take the account, I will acknowledge their pain, but insist we wait until every invoice factored with Duefuss is paid and no buyout is involved.

I will also listen to my instincts when I sense a client is going to do something devious, and I will pay very close attention to everything any AP person says about a client. There is nothing about this experience I want to relive, and actually felt somewhat fortunate that my loss was limited to $10,000.

The only silver lining: I have the satisfaction that Rufus Duefuss had his bell rung by my collection attorney.

Comment

Like Case Study 22 (Smuggley, Swindol & Finkbottom Finance), this one illustrates how untrustworthy and difficult some factors are. While Don had to deal with a completely unethical colleague, I dealt with one who was unbelievably incompetent.

A factoring company's longevity means absolutely nothing when it comes to providing good service, fair rates and practices, and ability to simply do the job. Duefuss, Inept, and Pathetic, Inc. clearly had been resting on their laurels far too long, and had long outlived their effectiveness as a factor. Every company needs to stay on the cutting edge of their industry to remain sharp and competitive. If they don't, ending up like Duefuss can be the result. (In case you're wondering – yes, DIPI is still very much in business.)

This case study is yet another lesson (when short payments happen, especially consistently) in asking the *debtor* why they haven't paid the invoice in full or at all. Don't ask the client and expect a truthful answer when you are already suspicious of him. Further, don't just use escrow reserves to recoup your advances and discounts, and consider the matter settled. If there is a consistent reason why invoices aren't paid in full, the sooner you know the real reason why – from the debtor – the better.

All too often, the reason you're not being paid properly is because a dishonest client is defrauding you. Unfortunately, he can quickly pull a very sneaky trick like Damon did and disappear, never to be seen again.

29.

Battleground Janitorial

Jeff Callender
Dash Point Financial

This is another case study – like the previous one, Damon Deevyus, LLC – with elements that are almost hard to believe. But as we all know, truth is often stranger than fiction. The incredible twists and turns with this client, if they hadn't happened to me, would make me think they couldn't be true. But everything in this case absolutely happened, and I can't imagine they could ever happen again to me or anybody else.

Battleground Janitorial was located in a neighboring town and was referred by my accountant, Knute Resolute. Knute has done my taxes for years and I trust him implicitly. He is also one of those rare accountants who actually understands and appreciates factoring and doesn't bad-mouth it. He has given me a few referrals over the years, and I have always enjoyed working with him. He's a good man.

Victor Major, another tax client of Knute, had recently bought Battleground Janitorial. Victor was in his early 70's and had led a storied life. A Special Forces Green Beret in Vietnam, he was a highly decorated war hero. In fact, his actions were so impressive that a book had been written about him and his valor during action in the war. Even more, a Hollywood studio was interested in purchasing film rights to the book, and plans were in the works to get the movie under way once the rights were purchased and all the legal paperwork completed.

Victor received some royalties from book sales though the amount wasn't that much; however what he would make from the movie rights once that happened (which dragged on for many months) was to be sizeable. But until those funds came in, he needed income like anyone else, which is why he purchased the janitorial company. Like most service company owners, Victor had receivables that took about 30 – 45 days to pay which made meeting payroll and expenses a challenge, at least until his ship came in (so to speak). Knute recognized factoring was exactly what Victor needed, referred him to me, and we met in Knute's office to get acquainted and look at Victor's account.

The company had solid customers with about $40,000 in monthly receivables, which was more than I usually start with a new client. But because Knute had referred him I felt I was in a secure position. We agreed to my standard terms, prepared the paperwork, signed the contract, and were soon under way.

Some of the accounts paid promptly to our lock box as expected, but others dragged out longer. We continued to fund him based on the strength of the good payers, but the slower ones became a problem. When the slow invoices reached the recourse period, we started charging them back from escrow reserves but he didn't have enough to cover what we were owed. We were unclear why these debtors weren't paying. They didn't return our calls and we had to stop funding invoices to them.

We soon became suspicious that Victor had picked up the checks from these customers and deposited them. We again attempted to contact the customers and were finally informed that yes indeed, they had given the checks to Victor. I called to confront him and asked if he had picked up and banked the checks. Amazingly, he admitted he had, and actually acted as if he really didn't realize doing so was wrong.

I had to point out he had already been paid for this invoices from Dash Point when we provided advances, that he had assigned the payments to us, and therefore those payments were ours – not his. This clearly hadn't occurred to him and the light bulb very dimly started to go on that he now owed us for those invoices.

I realized at that moment that Victor had learned, as a soldier, to obey orders and did that extremely well. But as a civilian he apparently never learned to think and reason on his own. Our war hero may have been impressive on the battlefield, but as an astute businessman he was a peeled zero. Impressive life story, nice guy...but absolutely clueless.

I went to see Knute (who wasn't aware of the check conversions), and told him what happened. He shook his head sadly and agreed Victor had messed up big time. He called Victor to make clear this money had to be paid back, at which point Victor finally got the whole picture. In his mind, if Knute was saying this, it must be true. We stopped funding him and through Knute, Victor agreed to a workout arrangement in which we would be paid a couple thousand dollars each month. Unfortunately, at that point we were owed about $40,000, so the workout was going to take a few years. That's a long time to wait for someone with Victor's business "skills" to pay you back. But if the movie deal ever came through the funds would be there as a lump sum.

Shortly into the workout period, Victor learned he had cancer and was very ill. In fact, the cancer was quite advanced and he was given only about six months to live. Knute worked hard to get Victor's estate in order. He made sure Dash Point would be repaid from the estate and/or movie rights (if those ever happened), and while I was out a lot of money for the time being, I was confident Knute would make sure I was made whole eventually. After all, it was in his interest – since he had referred Victor in the first place, plus I was a tax client of his – to do so.

A few months went by and little happened. But then one day, a report on the local TV news told of a very bad, fatal single car accident on a nearby freeway that had backed up rush hour traffic for hours. Not at all unusual – traffic accidents happen all the time; I didn't think much about it. But the next day, Knute called and asked if I had heard about that accident. I said yes, and he said, "Well, here's some more news. Victor was the driver of that car. He's dead."

Stunned, many thoughts raced through my head. Was it really an accident? Had Victor chosen to commit suicide this way rather than die a slow and miserable death from his cancer? After all, he was a decorated soldier who'd want to die with his boots on, not in a hospital bed hooked up to IV's. How was his wife coping? What would happen to his business? And especially – how would this affect the considerable amount of money I was owed?

Knute and I discussed these, as he had asked himself the very same questions. In the course of the conversation he mentioned something unknown to me previously: Victor owed Knute for unpaid accounting services. In fact, Victor owed Knute about the same amount of money he owed me. Knute was every bit as interested in getting paid back as I was. He assured me we would get our money back, and he was in a very good position to make that happen. He was in regular contact with Victor's widow, Violet, and mentioned she was a very difficult woman. (We eventually called her "Vile" for short.) However Knute had enough leverage with her to make sure everything was paid back properly. I just had to sit tight and trust him to make it happen.

There was little for me to do for several months other than keep in touch and get updates from Knute. One day he called me with some very interesting news: Victor had taken out a $2,000,000 life insurance policy before he became sick, in order to provide for his wife once he was gone. Because he died in a car accident, the policy was required to pay Vile, and it was just a matter of time before the funds were disbursed. Knute made it extremely clear to her that she would have to pay him, me, and other debtors out of the proceeds of the insurance policy when the money finally arrived. However, it would go directly to her and he would have to convince her to pay these obligations. If she balked, getting our money could become difficult.

About a year later, she finally received the insurance money and as Knute predicted, Vile intended to keep it all. She told him so bluntly and said she had no intention of paying anyone. His patience with her intransigence about gone, he insinuated she would face litigation if she didn't pay what was owed – which considering the sum she received, was a relatively small portion of it. She finally relented and Knute told me to update the total Dash Point was owed, given the long delay in payment. I calculated the accrued discounts over the two years now I had waited, and the total owed came to about $54,000.

I gave the number (and calculations) to Knute who in turn gave it to Vile. She of course thought I was robbing her blind and let Knute know her thoughts in no uncertain terms. But he stuck to his guns and in a short time I received a check – as did Knute and the other debtors – for every penny we were owed. Vile still had plenty of money left to live the rest of her life in comfort, and Knute and I celebrated a victory that was a long time coming.

We pictured Victor smiling down on all of us too, and feeling better that everything had finally been made right. After all, despite his poor business aptitude, he was a decent man and after many years of marriage, knew exactly what Violet was like. Vile, that is.

Comment

When an account goes bad and remains unpaid for as long as this one did, it's very rare to not only get your money back, but get every penny you're owed including a large accrued discount. My ace in this game was Knute: he was in a position to exert leverage I never could have without paying a boatload of money to an attorney. What's more, the fact Knute was also owed money, I was his tax client, and he was relentless in pursuing our funds, resulted in an usually happy ending.

The circumstances surrounding Victor's demise – and his whole life for that matter – were truly unique. If many of the conditions in this case had not been in place (the fatal car accident, the life insurance policy, Knute being owed a considerable sum, the leverage he had, and his iron resolve to get us all paid), I'm sure this would have been a nasty write off. Instead, we celebrated a hard-won victory.

Ever since this experience, I have never minded for a single second paying my tax bill to Knute's firm. After all, he's *my* hero.

30.
Effective Fundraising

Jeff Callender
Dash Point Financial

Effective Fundraising, owned by Grant Getsit, is a client I've had for eight years who was referred by a broker. In business a number of years, Effective Fundraising has a very successful technique for school groups to raise money that he markets throughout the Midwest. His customers include high school sports teams, cheerleading squads, marching bands, booster clubs, PTAs, and other groups seeking to raise funds for uniforms, trips, and other purposes to promote their activities. Invoices are normally paid by the treasurer of a group, though a few are paid by the school district.

DD

Underwriting his customers is impossible: they are school organizations led by staff and parents, and thus have no commercial credit history. But Grant rightly said when we started these are responsible groups who very rarely don't pay their bills in full. If he has a problem with a school he simply doesn't sell to them again. Because of the relatively low invoice size, losses would be small if they occurred, and he could easily cover them with other invoices because of the overall good volume of his business. His own history was squeaky clean and I was quite comfortable funding him, especially because he started slowly with small volumes. He factors to cover his relatively high cost of postage during his busy season and for payroll.

DD

Grant is a bright man who has tweaked his business over the years to where it runs extremely efficiently and predictably. Once a school group becomes a customer (and he has a very large customer base), Grant provides a step-by-step fundraising program to raise money. The funds raised are obtained from numerous small donations from relatives, neighbors, and family friends of the students. These donors make pledges of typically $5 to $100 to support the cause, and Grant's system enables him to track every pledge and donation made. Over the course of a fundraising drive, which typically lasts a few months, Grant's program enables the groups to raise between $5,000 to $15,000.

When the drive is over, Grant earns a 30% commission of the total funds received. Since he knows exactly how much has been collected, he sends an invoice for his commission to the treasurer and includes a pre-printed payment envelope, with my lock box as the remittance address. These payments typically arrive between three weeks to two months after invoicing, while most arrive in four or five weeks. There is no reason they should take longer since the money has already been collected, and he is paid from proceeds by the treasurer. Invoices are typically about $1,500 to $5,000 in size.

When an invoice goes over 45 days, he has a staff person watching the receivables who very effectively follows up. As a result, few invoices go past 60 days and chargebacks due to 90-day recourse are rare. A steady escrow reserve balance is always there to cover the unusual chargebacks.

Because this is a seasonal business (he shuts down for the summer) factoring with a monthly minimum would not work for Grant. Since Dash Point doesn't charge monthly minimums, and we welcome very small volumes like he has during his ramping up and winding down months each year, we are a very good match. During the middle part of the school year when fundraising is in full swing, he needs a credit line of $50,000, which we provide. Our discount and advance rates are what we typically charge all clients.

This has been a long-term, enjoyable, and lucrative relationship for both of us. A former accountant, Grant not only understands and appreciates how factoring works and how to make the best use of it, he is very intrigued with it as a "finance guy." He is impressed with the returns I make (no need to calculate those for him!), though he holds no grudges as to what he pays. He realizes that even though factoring is more expensive than a bank loan, he likes its flexibility, that it allows him to maintain steady cash flow when he needs it, and he can pay his predictable costs. This in turn enables him to run a consistently profitable business year after year. Like most savvy business owners who factor, he simply considers it a normal business expense that is required to run his operation profitably and steadily.

Because Grant Getsit appreciates the nuances of factoring from both sides of the table, he has mentioned a few times he has considered becoming a small factor himself. While I hope he remains a client forever, I wouldn't be surprised if one day he starts taking on small factoring clients on the side. He's factored long enough and is smart enough to realize what it involves, is realistic about the time and capital required, and is careful enough that he would do it right.

Grant stands out from other clients in that he is a "money guy" who uses factoring to run his business as efficiently and profitably as possible – not because he's desperate for cash. While some clients realize the returns we factors make are impressive, Grant is one of the few clients I've had who has seriously entertained the notion of becoming a factor himself. He has the wherewithal to pull it off successfully.

Comment

This is a great client with which to finish our thirty case studies. Here is a man who simply gets the program from every angle, and makes it work to everyone's advantage. He is smart, organized, runs his business very efficiently, knows exactly what he's owed, and actually provides self-addressed envelopes for payment with the factor's address pre-printed on the envelopes! What's more, he has a skilled staff person chasing the few slow payers he has, doesn't begrudge the cost of factoring, and may even become a factor himself eventually.

Grant is certainly the kind of client any factor would love to have in his portfolio. I hope he stays in mine for a long, long time.

Part 3

Analysis

Assessment

As we review the mix of good and bad experiences described in these thirty case studies, several general observations can be made.

Good Clients and Bad Clients

We've seen a number of clients that are clearly good, and plenty that are indisputably bad. In the two charts below, a summary of the good clients' characteristics is in the first chart, and the bad client's characteristics in the second. Client examples of each positive or negative characteristic are provided. These charts provide a clear summary of what makes good clients good, and bad clients (too often) awful.

Good Clients

	Example		Company
Honest, trustworthy	Claire Stedfast	6	Claire's Repairs
	Stewart Stalwart	12	Stalwart Security
	Onin Barbells	23	OWIES
	Adelle Adept	27	Methodical Mfg.
Customers pay well	Arianna Artiste	1	Smallnhappy Graphic Arts
	Claire Stedfast	6	Claire's Repairs
	Ruby Dazzle	8	Razzle & Dazzle Mfg.
	Stewart Stalwart	12	Stalwart Security
	Candi Cotton	17	Lunch & Munch Staffing
	Clyde Dale	20	HAWLIT
	Jacob Jobber	21	Techie Trekker
	Fran Tic	25	Safensound Janitorial
	Darrell Adept	27	Methodical Mfg.
	Grant Getsit	30	Effective Fundraising

Good volume / income for factor	Claire Stedfast	6	Claire's Repairs
	Ruby Dazzle	8	Razzle & Dazzle Mfg.
	Candi Cotton	17	Lunch & Munch Staffing
	Jacob Jobber	21	Techie Trekker
	Fran Tic	25	Safensound Janitorial
	Darrell Adept	27	Methodical Mfg.
	Grant Getsit	30	Effective Fundraising
Factors regularly	Arianna Artiste	1	Smallnhappy Graphic Arts
	Ruby Dazzle	8	Razzle & Dazzle Mfg.
	Stewart Stalwart	12	Stalwart Security
	Garrett Gogetter	15	Gogetter Property Services
	Jacob Jobber	21	Techie Trekker
	Fran Tic	25	Safensound Janitorial
	Grant Getsit	30	Effective Fundraising
Low maintenance	Arianna Artiste	1	Smallnhappy Graphic Arts
	Ruby Dazzle	8	Razzle & Dazzle Manufacturing
	Stewart Stalwart	12	Stalwart Security
	Darrell Adept	27	Methodical Mfg.
	Grant Getsit	30	Effective Fundraising
Organized / dependable / good communicator	Arianna Artiste	1	Smallnhappy Graphic Arts
	Stewart Stalwart	12	Stalwart Security
	Garrett Gogetter	15	Gogetter Property Services
	Candi Cotton	17	Lunch & Munch Staffing
	Jacob Jobber	21	Techie Trekker
	Fran Tic	25	Safensound Janitorial
	Adelle Adept	27	Methodical Mfg.
	Grant Getsit	30	Effective Fundraising

Low risk	Arianna Artiste	1	Smallnhappy Graphic Arts
	Ruby Dazzle	8	Razzle & Dazzle Manufacturing
	Grant Getsit	30	Effective Fundraising
Owner factors to make company stronger	Stewart Stalwart	12	Stalwart Security
	Garrett Gogetter	15	Gogetter Property Services
	Candi Cotton	17	Lunch & Munch Staffing
	Fran Tic	25	Safensound Janitorial
	Darrell Adept	27	Methodical Mfg.
	Grant Getsit	30	Effective Fundraising
Smart business person	Candi Cotton	17	Lunch & Munch Staffing
	Darrell Adept	27	Methodical Mfg.
	Grant Getsit	30	Effective Fundraising
Calm / no drama	Stewart Stalwart	12	Stalwart Security
	Darrell Adept	27	Methodical Mfg.
	Grant Getsit	30	Effective Fundraising
Loyal / factor's advocate / provides referrals	Stewart Stalwart	12	Stalwart Security
	Garrett Gogetter	15	Gogetter Property Services
	Candi Cotton	17	Lunch & Munch Staffing
	Grant Getsit	30	Effective Fundraising
Effective collector	Jacob Jobber	21	Techie Trekker
	Grant Getsit	30	Effective Fundraising

Bad Clients

	Example		Company
Dishonest /	Jay Blahzay	2	Blahzay Auto Transport
unethical /	Dee Seetful	3	Dee Seetful and
thief			Associates
	Willy B. Wiley	4	Shifty Shuffles Staffing Services
	Harvey Hoodwinker	5	Hardluck Harvey's Homes
	Lem Ecollum	11	Budibuddy Metal Fabrication
	Grumbel Sloppee	14	Sloppee Properties
	Floyd Fibberlips	16	Audacity Cleaning Service
	Wrangle Clank	19	Clank Brothers Cable & Wiring
	Tank Hammerhed	22	Smuggley, Swindol & Finkbottom Finance
	Hyden Sneek	24	Mr. Scumbucket Janitorial Company
	Bligh Slimegall	26	Slimegall Medical Transport
	Damon Deevyus	28	Damon Deevyus, LLC
	Victor Major	29	Battleground Janitorial
Bad debtors:	Jay Blahzay	2	Blahzay Auto Transport
poor payers /	Dee Seetful	3	Dee Seetful and
ignore NOAs /			Associates
factor-	Harvey	5	Hardluck Harvey's
unfriendly /	Hoodwinker		Homes
undependable	Leon Little	7	Smallfrey Alarm Systems
	Viki Tim	9	Dunfore Day Care
	Lem Ecollum	11	Budibuddy Metal Fabrication
	Floyd Fibberlips	16	Audacity Cleaning Service
	Damon Deevyus	28	Damon Deevyus, LLC

	Victor Major	29	Battleground Janitorial
High maintenance	Harvey Hoodwinker	5	Hardluck Harvey's Homes
	Grumbel Sloppee	14	Sloppee Properties
Disorganized / undependable / poor communicator	Willy B. Wiley	4	Shifty Shuffles Staffing Services
	Harvey Hoodwinker	5	Hardluck Harvey's Homes
	Tess Messner	10	Messner Janitorial Company
	Grumbel Sloppee	14	Sloppee Properties
High risk	Tess Messner	10	Messner Janitorial Company
	Lem Ecollum	11	Budibuddy Metal Fabrication
Factors ARs in desperation	Tess Messner	10	Messner Janitorial Company
	Wrangle Clank	19	Clank Brothers Wiring and Cable
Bad business decisions / clueless	Tess Messner	10	Messner Janitorial Company
	Dorrie Nobb	18	Dorrie Nobb Advertising
	Victor Major	29	Battleground Janitorial
Emotional / unpredictable	Wrangle Clank	14	Clank Brothers Wiring and Cable
	Grumbel Sloppee	19	Sloppee Properties
	Hyden Sneek	24	Mr. Scumbucket Janitorial Co.
Poor / ineffective /	Dee Seetful	3	Dee Seetful and Associates

untrustworthy collector	Lem Ecollum	11	Budibuddy Metal Fabrication
	Grumbel Sloppee	14	Sloppee Properties
	Wrangle Clank	19	Clank Brothers Cable & Wiring
	Hyden Sneek	24	Mr. Scumbucket Janitorial Company
	Damon Deevyus	28	Damon Deevyus, LLC
	Victor Major	29	Battleground Janitorial

Of the bad clients, those who intentionally did something wrong, deceitful, or unethical were:

Jay Blahzay	2	Blahzay Auto Transport
Dee Seetful	3	Dee Seetful and Associates
Willy B. Wiley	4	Shifty Shuffles Staffing Services
Harvey Hoodwinker	5	Hardluck Harvey's Homes
Lem Ecollum	11	Budibuddy Metal Fabrication
Grumbel Sloppee	14	Sloppee Properties
Floyd Fibberlips	16	Audacity Cleaning Service
Wrangle Clank	19	Clank Brothers Cable & Wiring
Tank Hammerhed	22	Smuggley, Swindol & Finkbottom Finance
Hyden Sneek	24	Mr. Scumbucket Janitorial Company
Bligh Slimegall	26	Slimegall Medical Transport
Damon Deevyus	28	Damon Deevyus, LLC

Not all the bad experiences were the clients' doing. Those who did not intentionally do anything wrong, yet whose circumstances left the factor with a lighter wallet, included:

Leon Little	7	Smallfrey Alarm Company
Viki Tim	9	Dunfore Day Care
Greg Goodfellow	13	Misfit Publishing Company

Factors' Vulnerability

A representative from my collection agency once said that factors are among the most frequently defrauded businesses in the country. He ought to know – he's been working in the industry for several years and has several factors as clients. He's seen it all; the case studies in this book are simply reflective of his (and the contributors') encounters.

While new factors' inexperience can result in some unpleasant events due to rookie mistakes and perhaps being too trusting, none of the contributors to this book are new factors. In other words, bad things can happen to good factors no matter how long they've been in business. What's more, even clients who have been honest and factored successfully for years can quietly change their stripes – especially when a tempting opportunity presents itself.

In the example of Case Study 24, Mr. Scumbucket Janitorial Company, Hyden Sneek had been factoring smoothly and without incident for years before he began to "borrow" from checks paying factored invoices and lie about it. In his case, the temptation was just too great to have every check pass through his hands before sending it to his factor.

No doubt his funny business started when things were a little tight one month and he took a shortcut to solve his problem. Unfortunately, he found how simple it was to take advantage of his factor's trust and soon made a habit of it. Things spiraled out of control from there.

Not providing such a temptation in the first place should be standard operating procedure for any factoring company. All payments *must* come directly to you, the factor, as the normal course of business. Period. Believe me, you don't want to have to deal with a Hyden Sneek of your own.

This is also a good reason to continue to maintain low exposures, never let your guard down, and never assume your procedures make you invincible. Factoring involves risk;

therefore you must follow specific strategies to minimize your risk at all times.

As you can see, the factoring landscape is littered with land mines, and risks lurk under even the most innocent-looking stones. Factors are constantly vulnerable to client dishonesty, poor management, customer ineptitude, and the unexpected "stuff" that ordinary life includes. Add to this many common mistakes factors can make without realizing it, and you can see why factors earn the higher rates they do: it's a matter of compensating for the risks they take every day.

Factors' Mistakes

How to Run a Small Factoring Business (Book 3 of The Small Factor Series) contains a chapter entitled "Common Mistakes." This chapter lists twenty-four errors often made by both new and experienced small factors. Of these twenty-four, ten are evident here in *Factoring Case Studies*. Some were made by the contributors, while others were made by previous factors the clients were trying to shed.

Below is a list of these ten mistakes made and the Case Studies in which they occured.

Common Mistake		Case Study
Complicated or Misleading Rates	8	Razzle & Dazzle Manufacturing
	28	Damon Deevyus, LLC
Being Rushed	10	Messner Janitorial Company
	19	Clank Brothers Wiring and Cable
Giving Advances for Work Not Completed	10	Messner Janitorial Company
	11	Budibuddy Metal Fabrication
	14	Sloppee Properties
	19	Clank Brothers Wiring and Cable
Blindly Batching Invoices	26	Slimegall Medical Transport
Not Saying "No"	9	Dunfore Day Care
	19	Clank Bros. Wiring and Cable
Debtor payments not sent to the factor (allowed by factor or re-routed / deposited by client)	2	Blahzay Auto Transport
	3	Dee Seetful & Associates
	4	Shifty Shuffles Staffing Services
	5	Hardluck Harvey's Homes
	16	Audacity Cleaning Services
	19	Clank Brothers Wiring and Cable
	24	Mr. Scumbucket Janitorial Company
	26	Slimegall Medical Transport
	28	Damon Deevyus, LLC
	29	Battleground Janitorial

Poor Follow-up on Late- and Non-Payers	11	Budibuddy Metal Fabrication
	24	Mr. Scumbucket Janitorial Company
	26	Slimegall Medical Transport
Over Concentrations and Lack of Limits	19	Clank Brothers Wiring and Cable
	25	Safensound Janitorial and Maintenance
Letting Down Your Guard	19	Clank Brothers Wiring and Cable
	24	Mr. Scumbucket Janitorial Company
	26	Slimegall Medical Transport
Not Following Your Own Rules	11	Budibuddy Metal Fabrication
	19	Clank Brothers Wiring and Cable

Risk Minimization Strategies

Fundamentals for Factors discusses four general strategies for minimizing risk. To some degree they are the antithesis of the mistakes mentioned above. The strategies and their sub-points are:

1) Set Financial Limits
2) Determine Receivables You Will and Will Not Factor
3) Perform Adequate Due Diligence
   a) Client Due Diligence
   b) Customer Due Diligence
   c) New Invoice Due Diligence
   d) Overdue Invoice Due Diligence
4) Establish and Build Up Reserves

This book has been filled with examples which put these strategies into practice, particularly numbers 1, 3 and 4. When these strategies were not faithfully practiced, problems usually resulted.

Several case studies point to the value of performing proper due diligence, particularly strategy 3c and 3d. Verify invoices to make sure the product or service has been received and payment will be made to the factor's address. Many of the bad experiences resulted because the factors neglected these verifications. Other problems resulted from waiting too long to follow up on late invoices.

We've seen the numerous risks that go with factoring – dishonest, selfish, careless, and otherwise untrustworthy clients and customers, and errors in procedures or judgment made by factors. Therefore common sense suggests a factor's foremost strategy is to set financial limits, thereby putting limited amounts at risk. This is especially prudent when the factor is new, even if his or her pool of factoring funds is sizeable.

The most important risk minimization strategy is to avoid over-concentration. Following normal due diligence and standard factoring practices will lessen the chance of fraud, loss from client errors, loss from mistakes by the factor, and so on. But your greatest weapon for avoiding a catastrophic loss is a simple, cost-free procedure: set credit limits with clients and customers, and limit the size of invoices you buy. Then *stay within these limits and do not make exceptions.* If you increase a client's credit limit, do so in relatively small increments only after clients have proven to be honest and customers payments have proven to be dependable.

Further, set an absolute ceiling which no client's credit limit will exceed. If a client outgrows this limit, broker him to a larger factor and continue to earn commissions, or participate with another factor and share the income (and risk).

While using this strategy will not prevent losses, you will avoid catastrophic events fatal to your business. This is the simplest yet most often overlooked (or ignored) risk management tool that any factor can employ.

The Core of Factoring: People

When all the risks are taken into account and protective measures are in place, we come back to the human element at the core of factoring. Factors deal with finances and business procedures, but everything comes down to human interactions. These relations involve reciprocal trust and working together for mutual benefit. When these positive attributes are in place and potential hazards overcome, the practice of factoring works, and works extremely well. The results are financially quite rewarding and emotionally very satisfying.

Consider the most successful case studies we've seen:

	Case Study Name	Mark of Success
1	Smallnhappy Graphic Arts	Client does what she enjoys and is financially stable.
8	Razzle & Dazzle Manufacturing	Factoring helped a small business grow and created good income for the factor, client, and broker.
12	Stalwart Security	Long-term stable business due to factoring.
15	Gogetter Property Services	Factoring helped the client get his business established and grow steadily.
17	Lunch & Munch Staffing	Factoring helped the business grow and become successful.
21	Techie Trekker	Factoring stabilized business and personal cash flow for a one-person business.
25	Safensound Janitorial and Maintenance	Anchor client for factor; factoring helped them become bankable.
30	Effective Fundraising	Factoring made business as efficient and profitable as possible.

Yes, factoring can be risky. Factoring can also be extremely rewarding when you work with good people, know you are providing a much-needed service, follow sound business practices, and make a very high return on investment.

As these case studies have shown, factoring is an intensely people-centered business. Factoring certainly involves business financing, but it is far more than that. Factoring is relationships. Factoring requires trust while demanding street smarts. Factoring requires common sense. Factoring brings out the very best and the very worst in people.

If you are highly risk-averse, factoring is not for you. If you are motivated solely by profit, you will not be a good factor, you will neither deserve nor earn your clients' loyalty, and you will not enjoy the people with whom you work. If you go into factoring only to help people, your good intentions will get slaughtered and your sense of innocence shredded.

Those who lack the right perspective or are careless don't stay in factoring. You'll learn of these as you spend time in this field. However, factors who run their operations properly, show sound judgment, use common sense, make excellent income, and help many businesses, tend to stick around.

These are the people who enjoy the rewards of factoring for a very long time. If you factor with a realistic approach, a cautious attitude, and a desire to improve your clients' lives as well as your own, you will find factoring a fascinating and rewarding business.

Part 4

Appendix

Reference Charts

So that you may easily find and refer to the case studies in this book, the following charts will help you find a particular case study easily. They are sorted by:

1. Case Study Number

2. Contributor Names

3. Case Study Names

4. Primary Character Names

5. Other Character Names

#	Case Study Name	Contributor
1	Smallnhappy Graphic Arts	Jeff Callender
2	Blahzay Auto Transport	Don D'Ambrosio
3	Dee Seetful & Associates	Jeff Callender
4	Shifty Shuffles Staffing Services	Rodrigo Riadi
5	Hardluck Harvey's Homes	Tony Neglia
6	Claire's Repairs	Jeff Callender
7	Smallfrey Alarm Company	Don D'Ambrosio
8	Razzle & Dazzle Manufacturing	Darrell Fleck
9	Dunfore Day Care	Jeff Callender
10	Messner Janitorial Company	Kim Deveney
11	Budibuddy Metal Fabrication	Ryan Jaskiewicz
12	Stalwart Security	Jeff Callender
13	Misfit Publishing Company	Melissa Donald
14	Sloppee Properties	Jeff Callender
15	Gogetter Property Services	Jeff Callender
16	Audacity Cleaning Services	Tony Neglia
17	Lunch & Munch Staffing	Kim Deveney
18	Dorrie Nobb Advertising	Tony Neglia
19	Clank Brothers Wiring and Cable	Melissa Donald
20	Hemisphere and World Logistics International Transfer (HAWLIT)	Rodrigo Riadi
21	Techie Trekker	Jeff Callender
22	Smuggley, Swindol & Finkbottom Finance	Don D'Ambrosio
23	Onin's Workouts & Isometric Exercise Systems (OWIES)	Rodrigo Riadi
24	Mr. Scumbucket Janitorial	Jeff Callender
25	Safensound Janitorial and Maintenance	Melissa Donald
26	Slimegall Medical Transport	Jeff Callender
27	Methodical Manufacturing	Jeff Callender
28	Damon Deevyus, LLC	Jeff Callender
29	Battleground Janitorial	Jeff Callender
30	Effective Fundraising	Jeff Callender

Contributor			Case Study Name
Jeff	Callender	1	Smallnhappy Graphic Arts
Jeff	Callender	3	Dee Seetful & Associates
Jeff	Callender	6	Claire's Repairs
Jeff	Callender	9	Dunfore Day Care
Jeff	Callender	12	Stalwart Security
Jeff	Callender	14	Sloppee Properties
Jeff	Callender	15	Gogetter Property Services
Jeff	Callender	21	Techie Trekker
Jeff	Callender	24	Mr. Scumbucket Janitorial
Jeff	Callender	26	Slimegall Medical Transport
Jeff	Callender	27	Methodical Manufacturing
Jeff	Callender	28	Damon Deevyus, LLC
Jeff	Callender	29	Battleground Janitorial
Jeff	Callender	30	Effective Fundraising
Don	D'Ambrosio	2	Blahzay Auto Transport
Don	D'Ambrosio	7	Smallfrey Alarm Company
Don	D'Ambrosio	22	Smuggley, Swindol & Finkbottom Finance
Kim	Deveney	10	Messner Janitorial Company
Kim	Deveney	17	Lunch & Munch Staffing
Melissa	Donald	13	Misfit Publishing Company
Melissa	Donald	19	Clank Brothers Wiring and Cable
Melissa	Donald	25	Safensound Janitorial and Maintenance
Darrell	Fleck	8	Razzle & Dazzle Manufacturing
Ryan	Jaskiewicz	11	Budibuddy Metal Fabrication
Tony	Neglia	5	Hardluck Harvey's Homes
Tony	Neglia	16	Audacity Cleaning Services
Tony	Neglia	18	Dorrie Nobb Advertising
Rodrigo	Riadi	4	Shifty Shuffles Staffing Services
Rodrigo	Riadi	20	Hemisphere and World Logistics International Transfer (HAWLIT)
Rodrigo	Riadi	23	Onin's Workouts & Isometric Exercise Systems (OWIES)

Case Study Name	#	Contributor
Audacity Cleaning Services	16	Tony Neglia
Battleground Janitorial	29	Jeff Callender
Blahzay Auto Transport	2	Don D'Ambrosio
Budibuddy Metal Fabrication	11	Ryan Jaskiewicz
Claire's Repairs	6	Jeff Callender
Clank Brothers Wiring and Cable	19	Melissa Donald
Damon Deevyus, LLC	28	Jeff Callender
Dee Seetful & Associates	3	Jeff Callender
Dorrie Nobb Advertising	18	Tony Neglia
Dunfore Day Care	9	Jeff Callender
Effective Fundraising	30	Jeff Callender
Gogetter Property Services	15	Jeff Callender
Hardluck Harvey's Homes	5	Tony Neglia
Hemisphere and World Logistics International Transfer (HAWLIT)	20	Rodrigo Riadi
Lunch & Munch Staffing	17	Kim Deveney
Messner Janitorial Company	10	Kim Deveney
Methodical Manufacturing	27	Jeff Callender
Misfit Publishing Company	13	Melissa Donald
Mr. Scumbucket Janitorial	24	Jeff Callender
Onin's Workouts & Isometric Exercise Systems (OWIES)	23	Rodrigo Riadi
Razzle & Dazzle Manufacturing	8	Darrell Fleck
Safensound Janitorial and Maintenance	25	Melissa Donald
Shifty Shuffles Staffing Services	4	Rodrigo Riadi
Slimegall Medical Transport	26	Jeff Callender
Sloppee Properties	14	Jeff Callender
Smallfrey Alarm Company	7	Don D'Ambrosio
Smallnhappy Graphic Arts	1	Jeff Callender
Smuggley, Swindol & Finkbottom Finance	22	Don D'Ambrosio
Stalwart Security	12	Jeff Callender
Techie Trekker	21	Jeff Callender

Primary Character		Case Study Name	Contributor
Arianna Artiste	1	Smallnhappy Graphic Arts	Jeff Callender
Bligh Slimegall	26	Slimegall Medical Transport	Jeff Callender
Candi Cotton	17	Lunch & Munch Staffing	Kim Deveney
Claire Stedfast	6	Claire's Repairs	Jeff Callender
Clyde Dale	20	Hemisphere and World Logistics International Transfer (HAWLIT)	Rodrigo Riadi
Damon Deevyus	28	Damon Deevyus, LLC	Jeff Callender
Darrell Adept	27	Methodical Manufacturing	Jeff Callender
Dee Seetful	3	Dee Seetful and Associates	Jeff Callender
Dorrie Nobb	18	Dorrie Nobb Advertising	Tony Neglia
Dusty Dazzle	8	Razzle & Dazzle Manufacturing	Darrell Fleck
Fess Messner	10	Messner Janitorial Company	Kim Deveney
Floyd Fibberlips	16	Audacity Cleaning Services	Tony Neglia
Garrett Gogetter	15	Gogetter Property Services	Jeff Callender
Greg Getsit	30	Effective Fundraising	Jeff Callender
Greg Goodfellow	13	Misfit Publishing Company	Melissa Donald
Gretta Goodfellow	13	Misfit Publishing Company	Melissa Donald
Grumbel Sloppee	14	Sloppee Properties	Jeff Callender
Harvey Hoodwinker	5	Hardluck Harvey's Homes	Tony Neglia
Hyden Sneek	24	Mr. Scumbucket Janitorial	Jeff Callender
Jacob Jobber	21	Techie Trekker	Jeff Callender
Jay Blahzay	2	Blahzay Auto Transport	Don D'Ambrosio
Lem Ecollum	11	Budibuddy Metal	Ryan Jaskiewicz

		Fabrication	
Leon Little	7	Smallfrey Alarm Company	Don D'Ambrosio
Fran Tic	25	Safensound Janitorial and Maintenance	Melissa Donald
Onin Barbells	23	Onin's Workouts & Isometric Exercise Systems (OWIES)	Rodrigo Riadi
Ruby Dazzle	8	Razzle & Dazzle Manufacturing	Darrell Fleck
Rusty Razzle	8	Razzle & Dazzle Manufacturing	Darrell Fleck
Stewart Stalwart	12	Stalwart Security	Jeff Callender
Tank Hammerhed	22	Smuggley, Swindol & Finkbottom Finance	Don D'Ambrosio
Viki Tim	9	Dunfore Day Care	Jeff Callender
Victor Major	29	Battleground Janitorial	Jeff Callender
Willie B. Wiley	4	Shifty Shuffles Staffing Services	Rodrigo Riadi
Wrangle Clank	19	Clank Brothers Wiring and Cable	Melissa Donald

Other Characters	Relationship	#	Case Study Name
Adelle Adept	Office manager	27	Methodical Manufacturing
Big Volume Wholesale	Customer	13	Misfit Publishing Company
Buymyhy Tech Products	Client	22	Smuggley, Swindol & Finkbottom Finance
Chelsea Checkonum	State consultant for New Hampshire	5	Hardluck Harvey's Homes
Cleaver Squeezem	Collection attorney for Dash Point Financial	3	Dee Seetful and Associates
Cleaver Squeezem	Collection attorney for Dash Point Financial	14	Sloppee Properties
Cleaver Squeezem	Collection attorney for Dash Point Financial	24	Mr. Scumbucket Janitorial Company
Cleaver Squeezem	Collection attorney for Dash Point Financial	26	Slimegall Medical Transport
Conrad Clientshield	Attorney for Coveryerbutt Construction	16	Audacity Cleaning Service
Coveryerbutt Construction	Customer	16	Audacity Cleaning Service
D.L. Phinder	Broker	22	Smuggley, Swindol & Finkbottom Finance
D'Lay, Obstrukt & Hindir (DOH)	Attorney firm for Mr. Scumbucket	24	Mr. Scumbucket Janitorial Company
Dinkyrink Development	Customer	3	Dee Seetful and Associates
Dudley Deevyus	Father of Damon Deevyus	28	Damon Deevyus, LLC
Duefuss, Inept & Pathetic, Inc. (DIPI)	Previous factor for Damon Deevyus	28	Damon Deevyus, LLC
Easley Foold Nursing Facility	Customer	4	Shifty Shuffles Staffing Service
Enlightened Property Managers	Customer	15	Gogetter Property Services
Erren Oopsie	Office Manager for Oxygen Funding	22	Smuggley, Swindol & Finkbottom Finance
Flakey Systems Corporation	Customer	28	Damon Deevyus, LLC
Fletcher Flunkey	AP clerk	26	Slimegall Medical Transport
Merv S. Tic	Husband of Fran Tic	25	Safensound Janitorial

			and Maintenance
Fritz Findsem	Broker	24	Mr. Scumbucket Janitorial Company
Gilbert Glibwerds	Salesperson for Smuggley	22	Smuggley, Swindol & Finkbottom Finance
Giterdun Payment Services	Payment service for customer	23	Onin's Workout & Isometric Exercise Systems (OWIES)
Goodsnstuff International	Customer	20	Hemisphere and World Logistics International Transfer (HAWLIT)
Hector D. Tekter	Broker	11	Budibuddy Metal Fabrication
Housing and Land Property Restorations (HLPR)	Customer	14	Sloppee Properties
Housing and Land Property Restorations (HLPR)	Customer	15	Gogetter Property Services
Ima Patsy	Owner of Phonyphront, Inc.	4	Shifty Shuffles Staffing Service
Jean Clank	Wife of Wrangle Clank	19	Clank Brothers Wiring and Cable
Knute Resolute	Accountant for Dash Point Financial	29	Battleground Janitorial
Les Messner	Son of Fess & Tess Messner	10	Messner Janitorial Company
Lizzy Toobizy	Owner of Dinkyrink Development	3	Dee Seetful and Associates
Makesfurem Manufacturing	Manufacturer	8	Razzle & Dazzle Manufacturing
Marcie Mastiff	Receptionist at Dinkyrink Development	3	Dee Seetful and Associates
Miley Wiley	Mother of Willie B. Wiley	4	Shifty Shuffles Staffing Service
Neville Knozsquatt	Attorney for Dinkyrink Development	3	Dee Seetful and Associates
Obfuscation Fitness and Training	Customer	23	Onin's Workout & Isometric Exercise

(OFAT)			Systems (OWIES)
Onus, Dred & Trembal	Collection agency for Dash Point Financial	3	Dee Seetful and Associates
Onus, Dred & Trembal	Collection agency for Dash Point Financial	14	Sloppee Properties
Onus, Dred & Trembal	Collection agency for Dash Point Financial	26	Slimegall Medical Transport
Onus, Dred & Trembal	Collection agency for Dash Point Financial	28	Damon Deevyus, LLC
Payurides	Customer	26	Slimegall Medical Transport
Phonyphront, Inc.	Business used to deposit factored payments	4	Shifty Shuffles Staffing Service
Riley Wiley	Father of Willie B. Wiley	4	Shifty Shuffles Staffing Service
Rosa Thorne	AP rep at customer's office	19	Clank Brothers Wiring and Cable
Sheeda Boss	AP supervisor	26	Slimegall Medical Transport
Silverhair Financial	Broker's company	14	Sloppee Properties
Stickittooem & Bulleys	Attorneys for Stonewallen Megacorp	7	Smallfrey Alarm Company
Stonewallen Megacorp	Customer	7	Smallfrey Alarm Company
Tank Hammerhed	Supervisor of Gilbert Glibwerds	22	Smuggley, Swindol & Finkbottom Finance
Tenacious & Durble	Attorney firm for Dash Point Financial	24	Mr. Scumbucket Janitorial Company
Tess Messner	Wife of Fess Messner	10	Messner Janitorial Company
The Food Brood	Customer	17	Lunch & Munch Staffing
Tiff Clank	Brother of Wrangle Clank	19	Clank Brothers Wiring and Cable
Truman Tenacious	Attorney for Dash Point Financial	24	Mr. Scumbucket Janitorial Company
Unapproachable Property Management	Customer	15	Gogetter Property Services
Vail N. Obscurity	Broker	28	Damon Deevyus, LLC
Violet (Vile) Major	Wife of Victor Major	29	Battleground Janitorial
Whitefang and	Attorney firm for	11	Budibuddy Metal

Gnash	12five Capital		Fabrication
Whitney Whitefang	Attorney for 12five Capital	11	Budibuddy Metal Fabrication
Wilson Wizen	Broker	14	Sloppee Properties

Books and Ebooks by Jeff Callender

The Small Factor Series

Book 1
Factoring Wisdom:
A Preview of Buying Receivables

Short Sayings and Straight Talk
For New & Small Factors

Book 2
Fundamentals for Factors

How You Can Make
Large Returns in Small Receivables

Book 3
How to Run a
Small Factoring Business

Make Money in Little Deals
the Big Guys Brush Off

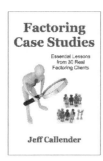

Book 4
***Factoring Case Studies
(2nd Edition)***

Essential Lessons from
30 Real Factoring Clients

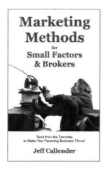

Book 5
***Marketing Methods
for Small Factors & Brokers***

Tools from the Trenches
To Make Your Factoring Business
Thrive!

About This Series

The Small Factor Series is designed to:

1. Provide a succinct introduction and summary of the books in this series as well as other writings by Jeff Callender.

2. Introduce readers to the investment of factoring small business receivables.

3. Provide a step-by-step manual with complete instructions for small factors.

4. Provide 30 real-life examples of factoring clients from the files of people who have been investing in small receivables for some time.

5. Describe and analyze numerous marketing methods to bring in new business which have been used by the eight contributors to the book.

Each book in the series is written to address the above points:

- Book 1, *Factoring Wisdom: A Preview of Buying Receivables,* introduces and summarizes the other books with brief excerpts from each, and arranges them by subject matter.

- Book 2, *Fundamentals for Factors* introduces potential factors to the business.

- Book 3, *How to Run a Small Factoring Business,* is the step-by-step manual.

- Book 4, *Factoring Case Studies* (2nd Edition), describes experiences of 30 real clients of small factors, which illustrate the many lessons and suggestions made in Books 2 and 3.

- Book 5, *Marketing Methods for Small Factors & Brokers*, includes contributions from seven small factors and an experienced broker.

Other Books by Jeff Callender

Factoring:
Sell Your Invoices Today,
Get Cash Tomorrow

How to Obtain Unlimited Funds
without a Loan

Written to introduce factoring to small business owners, this book compares factoring to traditional lending, shows how it can help a company's cash flow, and guides readers in determining if factoring can improve their business.

The above books are available in the following formats from DashPointPublishing.com:

- Paperback
- PDF
- Kindle
- iPad & Android

Ebooks by Jeff Callender

Accounting Methods for Factors and Their Clients

By Robert Vasquez and Jeff Callender

This ebook describes how to establish and maintain proper bookkeeping records for a factoring company and factoring clients. You'll learn how to use GAAP-approved procedures and make sure you're doing it right. Following these step-by-step instructions starts you on the right foot.

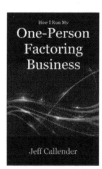

How I Run My One-Person Factoring Business

Want to get started running a small factoring business by yourself? This ebook shows how the author successfully began as a one-person operation, and the everyday tools you can use now to do the same.

How I Run My Virtual Factoring Office

A virtual office means you can work from just about anywhere you want. Learn the common tools and technology the author uses (available to anyone) to run his virtual factoring office. Enjoy the comforts of home – at work!

"Top 10" Ebooks by Jeff Callender
"Top 10" Ebooks for Factors:

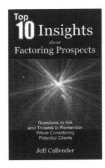

Top 10 Insights about Factoring Prospects

Questions to Ask
and Truisms to Remember
When Considering Potential Clients

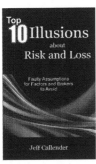

Top 10 Illusions about Risk and Loss

Faulty Assumptions for
Factors and Brokers to Avoid

Top 10 Statements You Never Want to Hear

Unwelcome Words for Factors
From or About Their Clients

10 Key Points to Look for in Factoring Software

Consider these 10 issues *before* purchasing software for your factoring operation

"Top 10" Ebooks for Clients:

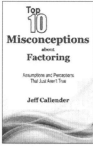

Top 10 Quotes on the Benefits of Factoring

Statements from Business Owners Who Factor Their Receivables

Top 10 Misconceptions about Factoring

Assumptions and Perceptions That Just Aren't True

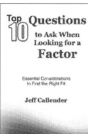

Top 10 Questions to Ask When Looking for a Factor

Essential Considerations to Find the Right Fit

Acknowledgments

I would like to thank the following people for the important parts they played in creating this book:

The **contributing writers** who generously gave their time, experiences, wisdom, and insights. Without them this book could not have been written.

Nicole Jones for her proofreading skills and creating the ebook versions of books in the Small Factor Series and all other titles, and making them available to the world.

Anne Gordon for her proofreading skills and valuable experience, comments, support, and adding the word "Unbelievable!!" to my factoring vocabulary...and this book.

Cover image credit: © sommersby/123RF.com
Cover image credit: © Sony Sivanandan/123RF.com
Cover image credit: © Dejan Jovanovic/123RF.com
Cover images arranged by Jeff Callender

Important Notice

Also by Jeff Callender

Paperbacks and Ebooks
The Small Factor Series includes 5 titles:

1. *Factoring Wisdom: A Preview of Buying Receivables*
   Short Sayings and Straight Talk for New & Small Factors   © 2012

2. *Fundamentals for Factors*
   How You Can Make Large Returns in Small Receivables   © 2012

3. *How to Run a Small Factoring Business*
   Make Money in Little Deals the Big Guys Brush Off   © 2012

4. *Factoring Case Studies*
   Essential Lessons from 30 Real Factoring Clients
   1st edition ©2003, 2005; 2nd edition © 2012

5. *Marketing Methods for Small Factors & Brokers*
   Tools from the Trenches to Make Your Factoring Business Thrive!   © 2012

Factoring: Sell Your Invoices Today, Get Cash Tomorrow
   How to Obtain Unlimited Funds without a Loan   © 2012

eBooks
For Factoring Clients:

Accounting Methods for Factors & Their Clients   © 2012
Top 10 Quotes on the Benefits of Factoring   © 2012
Top 10 Misconceptions about Factoring   © 2012
Top 10 Questions to Ask When Looking for a Factor   © 2012

For Factors:

Accounting Methods for Factors & Their Clients   © 2012
How I Run My One-Person Factoring Business   © 2008, 2012
How I Run My Virtual Factoring Office   © 2012
Top 10 Insights about Factoring Prospects   © 2008, 2012
Top 10 Illusions about Risk and Loss   © 2008, 2012
Top 10 Statements You Never Want to Hear   © 2008, 2012
10 Key Points to Look for in Factoring Software   © 2008, 2012

Spreadsheet Calculators
APR and Income Calculators   © 2002, 2012

Software
FactorFox Software   © 2006 – current year

Websites
www.DashPointPublishing.com   www.SmallFactor.com
www.DashPointFinancial.com   www.SmallFactorAcademy.com
www.FactorFox.com   www.FactorFind.com

About the Author

Jeff Callender had an unusual start to his business career. Though he is the son and grandson of businessmen, he began his working life as a pastor.

After earning a college degree in Sociology and a Master of Divinity degree, he served three churches in Washington state over 14 years. While he found ministry rewarding, he realized he had an entrepreneurial spirit which gradually pulled him toward business.

He left his career in the church and about a year later stumbled onto factoring. He began as a broker but after numerous referrals were declined only because of their small size, he started factoring very small clients himself. His career as a factor – and as a pioneer in the niche of very small receivables factoring – was thus born in 1994.

He has worked with a great number of very small business owners in need of factoring. He wrote his first book, *Factoring Small Receivables*, in 1995, and since then has written numerous books, ebooks, and articles, and spoken at many events in the factoring industry. His writing and two decades of experience have established him as a leading authority in the niche of small business factoring.

Jeff is the President of three companies he started. Dash Point Financial provides factoring services to small business owners throughout the U.S. It also provides the nucleus of his experience for writing. Learn more at DashPointFinancial.com.

Dash Point Publishing publishes and sells his books and ebooks, as well as those of other authors who write about factoring. His paperbacks are available from DashPointPublishing.com, as well as Amazon, the Kindle Store, Apple's iBookstore, and other online ebook sellers. Dash Point Publishing's website provides additional materials such as legal documents for smaller factoring companies.

FactorFox Software offers a cloud-based database solution for factors to track their client transactions. Originally based on his own company's back-office operational needs, readers of his books will feel right at home using the software in their own factoring companies. It has become one of the top platforms for the industry and is used by factoring companies throughout the world. More information can be found at FactorFox.com.

Having grown up in southern California, Jeff now lives in Tacoma, Washington with his wife, dog, and two cats. He has a grown son and daughter.

Made in the USA
Lexington, KY
28 January 2015